Rattlesnake Mesa

Rattlesnake Mesa

Stories from a Native American Childhood

BY EDNAH NEW RIDER WEBER

PHOTOGRAPHS BY RICHELA RENKUN

LEE & LOW BOOKS INC. • NEW YORK

ACKNOWLEDGMENTS

For Bunkie Butler: my friend, whose help with the typing has been invaluable. Thank you, Bunkie.

For Carolyn Grossman: my friend, who helped Naneh and Little Fat escape from the iron box where they had been held since 1964 . . . and who opened her beautiful foothills home for my first public reading. Thank you, Carolyn.

For Ramona: my daughter, who grew up hearing these stories told and retold in the traditional Native way . . . amid tears and laughter . . . by Aunties Minnie, Winona, and Rosie, who were there. So, now . . . it is time for me to pass these and the other stories I've put down to you, Ramona, to care for. This is truly your legacy and rich heritage. Thank you, Sun Dance Woman.

For Bill Weber: my husband of all these many years . . . for the enthusiastic support you've always given to me. Thank you, Vida.

For Jennifer Frantz: my editor, who has brought these children to you, with a fine insight into another time . . . and a different culture. For all your help. Thank you, Jennifer.   —E.N.R.W.

First I must thank Jennifer Frantz, our editor, for popping up like a crocus after a long winter. Your enthusiasm, patience, and vision made all things possible. Thank you to Lee & Low Books for seeing the beauty in the unusual. To Jan Reynolds for her miraculous timing and introductions. To my dear friend Jeff Troyer, a gentleman, scholar, adventurer, and sometimes Sherpa, I thank you for your loyalty, patience, and strong back—you will always be the "Best Man." And to the many other friends, family, and loved ones who have contributed to this book through their prayers, inspiration, favors, *mazaska*, love, and miracles: My amazingly handsome, talented, and infinitely supportive husband, John Fusco (Wakinyan Cante); my beautiful blue-eyed boy, Giovanni Fusco (Wakinyan Hoskila); my father, Richard T. Renkun; Jay Kennedy; Tiffany Michtem; the Children and Folks at the Westward Look. To Buddy Redbow, who loved bringing together people who needed to be together. I know wherever you are, you've had some kind of hand in all this—I hear you laughing! And humbly and forever to Tunkasila. *Pilamaya!*   —R.R.

Printed in Canada
Book design by Sylvia Frezzolini Severance
Book production by The Kids at Our House
The text is set in 12 point Sabon
10 9 8 7 6 5 4 3 2 1
FIRST EDITION

Library of Congress Cataloging-in-Publication Data
Weber, EdNah New Rider.
      Rattlesnake Mesa : stories from a native American childhood / by EdNah New Rider Weber ; photographs by Richela Renkun.— 1st ed.
            p. cm.
      ISBN 1-58430-231-3
      1. Weber, EdNah New Rider. 2. Pawnee girls—Biography. 3. Pawnee girls—Relocation—Arizona—Phoenix. 4. Pawnee girls—Education—Arizona—Phoenix. 5. Phoenix Indian School—History.
I. Title.
E99.P3W43 2004   979.1'7300497933'0092—dc22   2004002385

I DEDICATE THIS BOOK of memories to the Spirits of Native American children of all tribes who were torn from their families and put through hard labor and rigorous military training in United States Indian Schools throughout our own land. This then . . . is for your children, your grandchildren, and all others.

I give these stories . . . and through them may you look closer with pride . . . and great humility . . . at a time when the Indian people made yet another great struggle for survival by surrendering their precious children.

—E.N.R.W.

IN MEMORY OF MY Uncle Pete Rock (Che Nodin) full-blood Obijwa, naval commander, athlete, and alumnus of the Carlisle Indian School (1918–1990).

—R.R.

Contents

Homecoming

Foreword

The stories in this book are true.

They are from EdNah's past—things that happened when she was just a little girl—and she tells them just as she remembers them.

EdNah's stories reflect a time when America was very different from what it is today. EdNah grew up in the early 1900s. Not long before, Native Americans had fought wars against the United States government to defend their ancestral lands and traditional way of life. Many of the adults EdNah knew as a child remembered these days of war. Many of the grandfathers had even fought as warriors against U. S. soldiers.

When the Indian Wars ended, the Native American way of life was changed forever. Indian lands were taken over by the U. S. government. Tribes were gathered together, sometimes moved to other parts of the country, and forced to live on parcels of land called reservations.

The government also decided that Indian children such as EdNah should be sent away to boarding schools to be educated. These schools were often far from their reservations, and children did not see their families for nine months at a time, sometimes more. Indian parents did not have a choice about whether or not they sent their children to school. It was a law, and parents could suffer serious consequences if they did not obey. In some cases they could even go to jail.

At the schools the children were taught reading, writing, and arithmetic, as well as trades such as farming and blacksmithing for boys and cooking and sewing for girls. But the boarding schools also had another purpose—to change Native American children. Government officials believed schooling would "educate the Indian out of them," causing the children to give up their ancestors' traditional ways. The government hoped these Indian children would simply forget what it meant to be Indian.

But some things ran deeper than anyone could expect. Some things were buried, safely, deep in one's heart. And children like EdNah would not forget.

—*Richela Renkun*

I would climb the Mesa,
up that high mountain,
search under the giant pines,
if only I could find us again.

Crown
Point

Crown Point

Crown Point Indian Agency was like a tiny, precious jewel flung far out on the edge of the Eastern Navajo Reservation. It was set back in the cup of a mesa, like a horseshoe. In miles and miles of arid desert land sat this small, green oasis—a little Indian boarding school. Surrounded by tall trees, shrubbery, and flowers, it was tended with great care.

In March my Father picked me up from my Grandmother's home and brought me to Crown Point to live with him, finishing the school year.

My Aunt Elizabeth and Uncle Joe also lived here, employed in the Indian service. These people—Aunt Elizabeth, Uncle Joe, and my Father—were all strangers to me.

I was miserable. I did not want to be there. I did not want to live with this stranger . . . my Father. I didn't want any part of this life. I was at Crown Point because my beloved Grandmother, who had raised me from a baby, had taken her journey to the Spirit World. My heart was shattered. No one knows how a small child grieves . . . unable to express the intense anguish locked inside. Tears . . . tears . . . tears. Tears do not heal the broken heart.

The adults acted as if everything was just fine, as if nothing traumatic had just happened. They would talk in front of me . . . as if I blended into walls . . . as though I didn't have ears.

"How is she taking all this?"

"Oh, very well . . . children, you know."

"She's fine. She's just shy and quiet."

Very quiet . . . because small children cannot speak or express themselves about death.

Inside . . .

I longed for my cherished Grandmother.

Why couldn't I have traveled on with her to the Spirit World? Why didn't she take me on THIS journey? She'd taken me on so many others. I'd have been good . . . very good.

In my dreams she appeared and I'd cry out,

"Grandmother . . . Grandmother . . . wait . . . wait for me."

A tender smile would cross her beautiful face, and she'd be gone.

I was left alone . . . again.

~~~

At Crown Point there was a boarding school for Indian children from kindergarten through sixth grade. There were two dormitories for the girls and three for the boys. The girl students numbered around 150, the boys about 200. To maintain these children and keep the school running were a vast kitchen and dining hall. There was a bakery, a laundry, and a hospital. A powerhouse generated electricity for the school. There were employees working in all these departments. Mostly Anglos . . . some Indians.

Then there was the day school for the children of Crown Point employees, in which I found myself enrolled. I would finish the school year there. The next school year I would be sent to a boarding school in Phoenix.

The day school was a one-room schoolhouse with no more than ten students. The teacher, Miss Bonnie, taught all grades.

On my first day of school, a girl named Naneh came by my Father's place to take me to the schoolhouse. She already knew I was coming to Crown Point. Her family and my Father were close friends.

A boy named Little Fat joined us on the half-mile walk to school.

As with most children, there was no awkwardness in our first meeting. They told me about their school. They liked it, especially Miss Bonnie. They were in the second grade. I was seven-nearly-eight years old. Naneh and Little Fat were the same age as I.

We began walking to school together every day. When we got there, we'd play jump rope or jacks with the other children.

Miss Bonnie was young, and sometimes she played with us. Inside the schoolhouse she had all kinds of potted plants hanging in the windows. She kept a little fire going in the coal stove to take off the morning chill. The big room was bright and cheery.

I began to look forward to going to school; and Naneh, Little Fat, and I became fast friends. They asked no questions of my past . . . nor did they care. They lived in today and for tomorrow. My own life began changing, flowing right alongside theirs.

I learned it was possible to roll all the laughter and joy I shared with my Grandmother into a tiny ball and store it within my soul, where it would be forever safe and always near.

Smile, laugh a lot . . . cry little!

Rattlesnake Mesa

This Mesa called Rattlesnake was about a mile northwest from the Indian Agency, behind Boardman's Trading Post. It wasn't as high as the surrounding mesas. Climbing it was fairly easy.

The Navajos believed Rattlesnake Mesa to be the home of a giant Grandfather Rattlesnake and his family. The Mesa was split into a thin wedge. In this deep crevice is where the snakes lived, they said.

Everyone warned us, "Stay away from that Mesa. Don't go climbing there." We were told this again and again.

But . . . for Naneh, Little Fat, and me it had a special appeal. We were drawn to it. We could not help ourselves. We'd spend whole days up there. Never did we ever see a rattlesnake or any other kind of snake.

The point we claimed was flat and faced west. Toward the home of the Thunderbeings. Home of the Thunderbeings it certainly was.

Majestic. Alive. Electrifying!

Against the horizon here and there we'd

see long dark shadows of rain falling Earthward, like tattered spider-webs. Slashes of brilliant sunlight shining on red-orange mesas. Zigzag lightning streaking across the skies, too far away to hear their thunder. Small whirlwinds skittering this way and that way, like little cyclones. "Mothers-in-Law" our people called them.

As Naneh, Little Fat, and I gazed over the great land, our hearts were so filled with the serenity, beauty, and power of it . . . that . . . often we small children had no conversation.

Our eyes gave us memories—a magnificence to last a lifetime. This was our place. It was here that we left our marks forever! Here we scratched into rock our own legend. We inscribed our initials, our whole names. We chipped out our totems. Mine was a Flower, four petals lifting toward the Sun. Naneh and Little Fat did animals. Mine was always the same—a Flower, four petals toward the Sun.

We had seen pictographs and petroglyphs all over the reservation in special places. This rock art is a natural thing for children to do. It keeps you busy and interested because it's your ideas and your work. You may keep adding or if you need to change something, you merely erase it. To erase you use a flat rock and go over what you need to remove by rubbing. Just like using an eraser.

One particular summer day we had a big brainstorm. We decided to work together on one large petroglyph. We thought a rattlesnake was most appropriate. We quibbled over how long it should be, where we would put it. Naneh wanted it to be crawling westward as if it were crawling off the Mesa. Little Fat and I said it should be stretched out as if it were sleeping in the Sun. Now you know, when rattlesnakes sun themselves, they like to stretch straight out! Naneh agreed to that. In turn we said she could mark the length of it. We were thinking three feet or so, like most real snakes.

But nooooooo. Naneh started marking and marking. Our Snake was to be more than eight feet long! "Too long . . . too long . . . ," Little Fat and I protested loudly.

Naneh laughed at us, saying, "You said I could mark its length. . . . If we really are going to do this, then we should do some important art. Not just make a *worm!*"

Important art . . . We liked that!

Naneh was right.

Thus began many, many trips up Rattlesnake Mesa that summer. We were entirely serious about this project. We went up the Mesa each day, like going to a job. Nothing interfered with our work! Packing peanut butter sandwiches each morning, we were off for the day . . . not returning home until the 4:00 P.M. "Stop Work" whistle blew down at the Engine House.

It was then we'd quit whatever we were doing. We'd pick up our tools and hide them in a small crack, covering them with large rocks. We'd scramble back down Rattlesnake Mesa.

Each day we went up we made a little progress. . . . We could see it.

First we lightly scratched out a snake's body—exactly as long as Naneh wanted. Then a triangle head. About eighteen inches from the head we began the diamondback pattern, down the long back, three inches long and three inches wide. Twenty-three diamonds were scratched in. Very slowly our Rattlesnake began to take shape.

After the preliminary sketching we began our petroglyph in earnest.

We had tools—Little Fat, a broken butcher knife and big nails; Naneh, a long obsidian spearhead with a sharp point. I had a table knife and fork from my Auntie's kitchen. These wonderful gadgets were all we needed.

We spoke of the Ancient Ones. "Poor things," we said. "No good scratching tools. What all would they have drawn if they'd had big nails?"

As the days went by, our Snake became more intricate. We double-chiseled the lines on the diamonds. We pecked out scales starting from the head and stopping where the diamonds began.

Little Fat was always half lying down as he drew out his work, saying he could put more force into the pattern that way. We scratched deep into the sandstone.

"This handsome Snake will last forever. New people will think it's old, old. *Prehistoric.*" So we pecked even deeper. Yah, yah!

One day Naneh's older sister Biggi popped up over the Mesa. We could see what brought her . . . *curiosity!* Biggi had more class than anyone we knew. She was two years older than we, considering herself a grown-up already. She lived in books . . . not in life as we did. The more she read, the older she became. Biggi was very old. We paused in our work on the wonderful Snake. Big smiles of greetings on our faces.

"Ho, Biggi."

Someone of importance had arrived to view our art. In expectation we sat back on our heels . . . waiting for her approval and admiration of our Snake.

Biggi slowly circled our Snake, looking hard. Tossing back her beautiful dark hair, squishing her eyes . . . she became an Art Critic.

"Ughhhhhhh . . . This . . . is . . . *ugly.*"

"Ughhhhhhh . . . Its belly's *too big.* . . ."

"Did it swallow a deer?"

Her voice pitched higher in disgust.

"Ughhhhhhh . . . Are those *ears* on its head?"

She looked each of us in the eye.

"This is how you're wasting your summer . . . dillydallying . . . digging in sandstone? You . . . *crazies!*"

She whirled, vanishing off the Mesa. We could hear her hollering as she skidded down on the loose rocks. We didn't move. We couldn't. She'd stunned us with insults. We were crushed.

But not for long.

"She's jealous of our Snake," whispered Naneh.

"Ha! She wouldn't even know how to do what we've done." Little Fat.

"Who cares what she thinks. This is the best Snake ever." Me.

"Yeah, who cares what she says. This is our own handsome Snake. . . . We made it. . . . It's ours."

"This beautiful Snake will tell everybody who sees it that the Great Grandfather of all Rattlesnakes lives inside this Mesa."

The Snake bonded us closer.

Lizard Children

Reaching the top of Rattlesnake Mesa, we'd throw ourselves down, puffing and sweating, catching our breath from the hard climb up.

One time Little Fat threw himself down . . . declaring he was a Lizard . . . basking on the sun-warmed rock. Arms and legs extended out from his body. He said he really, really was a Lizard, rattling on and on about his relationship to the Lizard People. That he could travel anywhere he pleased. Regardless of how steep . . . or how deep. That he could jump from the top of the Mesa to the bottom . . . unscathed.

Because . . . he was a Lizard!

That he slept with one eye open, as Lizards did . . . and we should watch ourselves because he always knew what pranks we were up to. Blah . . . blah . . . blah.

Little Fat raved on and on. I thought he was funny. But Naneh had heard enough of his blather, and said to him, "I think you do belong to those Lizard People . . . because . . . your belly looks like it's chock-full of ants and bugs. But I've been watching you. . . . Both your eyes have been closed . . . AND . . . you keep moving. That's NOT lizardlike. Ptttttt . . . Who wants to be a Lizard anyway?"

Little Fat slowly rolled over and sat up, keeping his eyes on Naneh. "You are a Lizard."

"I am not. . . . Never . . . never."

Softly . . . he began baiting her. Staring her down. This was between those two. I was out of it.

"Oh yes . . . uh, huh . . . you are! You . . . have . . . big . . . ugly . . . scales."

"I do NOT. . . . I do NOT!"

Naneh could get mad really quickly. When she got mad, she'd cry. I thought she was going to cry.

Little Fat kept on.

"The scales are breaking through. . . . Looks like lizard skin to me!"

"Stop it. . . . Just stop it!" Naneh screeched.

Little Fat, loving this, continued. "You know, Naneh, your elbows . . . show your lizard blood. . . . See how scaly and dusty they are."

Naneh fell for it. Quickly turning over her arms, examining her elbows.

"They're chapped . . . just chapped! Do you hear? . . . Goofy!" Her screechy voice came down. . . . *Whew* . . . I was relieved. A big crisis had passed.

Flattening my body on the warm rock . . . I shrilled to the buzzards circling high above.

"I'm a Lizard! I'm a Lizard!"

Giggling, Naneh joined in. . . . "I'm a Lizard . . . I'm a Lizard . . . I have lizard elbows."

Little Fat, shaking with laughter . . . could barely holler, "We're Lizards. . . . We're Lizards!"

The Runaways

On a lovely Summer morning, Naneh, Little Fat, and I were sitting high up on Lone Butte. Scanning the valley below like young Eaglets.

Our keen eyes spotted Grey Eyes's team and wagon rounding Rattlesnake Mesa. Grey Eyes was easy to recognize. His teams of Horses were always beautifully matched. Today it was the blacks.

Grey Eyes had an unusual way of driving his team. He stood . . . feet planted far apart . . . ramrod straight behind the front seat of his wagon. The only other times we saw anyone do this was in the Wagon Races, where fearless drivers recklessly raced their teams against others.

Tall . . . athletic . . . Grey Eyes was a prominent sheep man. He came often to the Eastern Navajo Agency on business. Sheep business. He'd go to the Agency offices, complete his business there, then visit his cronies, the policemen at the Jailhouse. At noon he lunched in the Children's Dining Hall at the Boarding School, visiting with the children, the dishwashers, the cooks, the baker, before heading for home.

We watched Grey Eyes's arrival . . . the finding of shade for his Horses . . . the tying up of his team. We watched as he strode across the flats until the greenery of the Agency trees swallowed him up.

We sat discussing the beautiful way he handled his handsome team and wagon. How easy it must be . . . standing upright . . . driving his team . . . like driving a chariot. . . . It looked effortless . . . so smooth . . . so simple!

Suddenly, I don't know how it happened. . . . I swear to you. . . .

It happened so quickly. . . .

Naneh and I jumped up on the springboard seat. Little Fat took the reins, giving a click of his tongue and a slap of the reins across the Horses' haunches. He was standing behind the seat. Like Grey Eyes!

Driving Grey Eyes's team!

The team had a pleasant little walk, which turned into a frisky trot.

We went north up the road . . . passing Matchin's Trading Post . . . acting as though this spiffy rig belonged to us. We waved to the people outside the Trading Post, who were gaping and pointing at us in disbelief. Haskey Largo took off his big old Stetson hat . . . waving and hollering at us.

"Heyyyyyy . . . heyyyyyy!"

The mongrel dogs woke up, barking their stupid heads off. Customers ran out of the Post to see what the commotion was about.

Ohhh, Chindi! There was Old Lady Tsosie, whose tongue was as sharp as yucca blades. She was hollering loudly, pointing her green umbrella at us like a saber. "Nuuuuuuu. . . . Maybe . . . maybe . . . I'm not seeing what I'm seeing . . . before my eyes! Maybe . . . these are Shape Changers. . . . Nuuuuuu. . . . Maybe . . . *Witches*!"

"We'd better go back," Naneh suggested.

"I'm getting really scared," I said. It was seeing Old Lady Tsosie that scared me.

"All right, at the Well we'll turn," said Little Fat. He loved being driver of this outfit, still standing behind the front seat.

At the Well . . . hell broke loose.

Knowing Little Fat couldn't control them, the Horses tore into a run.

Galloping wildly . . . eyes bulging . . . they headed straight toward Pueblo Pintado, the worst road on the Reservation. Speeding in a cyclone of dirt and pebbles . . . we screamed at the top of our lungs.

"Whoa . . . Whoa. . . . Stop. . . . Whoa. . . . Stop!"

Afraid the wagon would overturn, crushing us to death. . . . *"Whoa . . . Whoa!"*

We cried to heaven like all sinners.

"Save us. . . . Help. . . . Save us!"

The Horses stopped. Just like that, they stopped. Frothing foam at their mouths. Sweat pouring from their bodies. We were half dead from the brutality of the runaway.

Naneh delirious . . . crying . . . crying.

Our voices were almost gone, our teeth nearly jarred out of our heads. We thought we were broken somewhere. Feeling for a bone sticking out someplace.

Naneh and I crawled to the back of the wagon. Sitting on the bare boards . . . rearranging our hair . . . spitting out dirt . . . wiping dust from our eyes. Really pitiful looking!

Little Fat regained his sense of propriety. Sitting himself on the springboard seat, reins in hand, clicking his tongue, he gently turned that wretched team around . . . heading home.

"It wasn't so bad," he said, turning to look at us. "You ninnies . . . yelling and screaming like fools. You scared the Horses. You're the ones who made it bad. You ought to see yourselves. . . . You look awful!"

I could barely croak, but I had to stop him.

"Hah! You don't look so great. Your face is caked with so much dust . . . only your eyeballs show!"

Naneh, giving her insult. "Your mother won't know you!"

We weren't talkative, and the Horses walked slowly on the return trip. Of course they did. . . . They were pooped from the runaway. As we again approached the Well, I worried what crazy thing they might do. But they kept walking.

There was still Matchin's Trading Post ahead. I was so ashamed. I tried to lie down, but the hard wagon boards hurt. To our relief, there were only a few small children and a couple of dogs playing in front of Matchin's.

Little Fat calmly returned Grey Eyes's team and wagon to their shady spot. Taking off his shirt, he wiped down the Horses. We deserved every bit of the pain and fright. No broken bones. Just bruised a lot.

Grey Eyes never said a word.

He knew.

We knew he knew.

Holy Smokes

Up the trail to Rattlesnake Mesa we discovered a small cave. It was big enough for Naneh, Little Fat, and me to move in comfortably, though we couldn't stand upright because the ceiling was too low. It was probably about four feet deep and six feet wide.

The Cave was our biggest secret. It was so secret we didn't call it by words. It had no name.

See . . . one time Auntie Elizabeth talked to us about words. She said that everything spoken went up . . . up . . . up into the atmosphere and got carried all over. That other people . . . maybe even in China . . . would know all your business. So be careful what you say, what you send up into the atmosphere.

Whenever we needed to mention the Cave to one another . . . we'd jerk our heads in that direction . . . with a knowing look . . . waving our eyebrows. . . . No words. 'Cause who knew . . . maybe we'd go there one day and there'd be a bunch of men from China sitting in our Cave! Just because we'd talked about it . . . said the words. And they'd grabbed them out of the atmosphere. Well, we weren't telling our secret business!

If we were on top of the Mesa and a Rain Cloud decided to empty itself real quick, we'd take shelter in the Cave. Or, if the Sun got too hot, we'd slide down into the coolness of the Cave, to rest awhile from the heat.

We also hid there to . . . SMOKE.

What we smoked was a flowerlike plant called Bee Weed. By mid summer Bee Weed bloomed profusely across the Flats. A stout plant with cornlike pods bursting open, delicately perfumed. Gorgeous purple in color. Amid the field of Bee Weed grew huge, brilliant yellow sunflowers, six to eight feet tall.

With warm lazy days and an abundance of flowers, the Bees swarmed in by the millions, attracted by the sweet nectar from the beautiful Bee Weed.

If you passed near and listened closely, you'd hear music like you've never imagined. The buzzing of the Bees sounded like a symphony of string instruments. Bees playing in wild crescendos . . . rising and falling . . . rising and falling.

One of Nature's great orchestras.

Naneh, Little Fat, and I crept up close, sitting on the ground. Very still. Listening as their synchronous music swelled, faded, and swelled again.

It was unbelievable! We didn't know of any other Winged Ones who played music like these Bees.

"Why?" we asked one another.

Because of the bountiful harvest?

The loveliness of the plants?

The privilege of sharing their work?

Ohhhhhh . . . that Bee Nation.

Fall . . . the flowers were gone.

Winter . . . stalks dried and golden.

Spring . . . rains and regrowth.

Summer . . . the Lizard Children arrived to collect dried stalks.

On the edge of the Plain, we began gathering dry pencil-sized stems.

Moving slowly . . . on Earth Mother . . . gently.

Shhhhhhhhh . . . the great Bee Symphony was in full performance. Butterflies of all colors, twinkling and twirling, sparkling with merriment. It was delightful.

Taking only what we needed, we quietly left. Crossing over and up Rattlesnake Mesa, we disappeared into the secret place.

Gleefully we spread out the dried stems, rubbing off the dry leaves and breaking the stems into pieces, six inches or so. With some baling wire we carefully poked the soft, spongy gunk out of the centers. If you poked too hard, you'd poke a hole through the side of the stem and it wouldn't be any good.

Laughing at our cleverness, we divided the stems.

For you . . . for you . . . for me.

Now it was time to light up and SMOKE. We pretended . . . these were cigarettes. We smoked . . . and spit . . . and smoked . . . and coughed . . . and smoked . . . and belched.

The smokes burned quickly . . . dry pith does, you know . . . tasting exactly like burning weeds smell. Well, that's what they were. Weeds. We didn't care. We had SMOKES!

Smiley

Smiley had been a Navajo Scout for the United States Army in his young man years. Now he was old, bent, and nearly blind.

My first memory of Smiley was seeing him come to the Agency for the pitiful rations the old scouts received, then watching him leave with his meager rations of beans, bacon, coffee, and salt tied in a burlap bag carried on his stooped back.

With small brisk steps, he returned to Hosky Butte miles away. Wiry and supple—and not much taller than I—he'd give us the army salute and be gone.

Countless times did we climb the mesas up, up to the higher Hosky Butte to Smiley's hogan, to visit with Smiley and Smiley's Wife. It was a long way to travel. There on top of the high Hosky Butte, under giant pristine pines, we rested.

Lounging on thick sheepskin pelts, we listened, enthralled by Smiley's stories in broken English, Navajo, and Spanish. Stories about when he was a scout, a tracker with a contingent of trackers from out of old Fort Defiance in the latter half of the nineteenth century.

Smiley told hair-raising stories about evil men . . . dangerous trails . . . men who just vanished and were never heard from again. His best stories were about trailing Apaches into old Mexico. We asked many silly, stupid questions. Smiley quietly disregarded them. He told us what he wanted us to hear—stories to sharpen our lives and our senses.

We listened and we watched.

Smiley's Wife was old too. She was small and thin, like a lovely slender reed, her grey hair pulled back in a chonga. Brown, wrinkled face, still very beautiful. It was her eyes, so alert and sparkling, that I was always drawn to. Spilling over with humor and laughter. In my mind I called her "Star Eyes." No wonder these two lived so long. . . . They enjoyed themselves.

Smiley's Wife busied about, mixing her tortilla dough, rolling small balls of it between her palms. With the dough resting, she pulled red-hot coals from the fire, and put the blackened coffeepot on them to simmer. Pulling more coals aside, she flattened them, preparing a bed to bake her tortillas on. When the coals were just right, Smiley's Wife would begin patting out her tortillas, flipping them to bake on top of the hot coals.

We were mesmerized . . . by Smiley's Wife.

When she finished, we ate ravenously of hot toasty tortillas brushed lightly with precious bacon drippings, sipping teeny sips of the hottest, blackest, most fragrant coffee ever.

Smiley and Smiley's Wife had no material goods. They had nothing. But . . .

They gave us comfort.

They told us truths.

They gave us food.

What gracious hospitality . . . to last a lifetime!

Skat Man

L ittle Fat was intrigued by Smiley's stories of the time he'd spent during the 1870s as one of the Navajo scouts for the United States Army.

Going home from our visits with Smiley, Little Fat imagined himself an Indian scout. Far away from his Company . . . spying . . . waiting . . . tracking . . . gathering information about the Enemy.

What Enemy?

Naneh and I . . . of course!

We played this game with the Great Tracker, Little Fat, on our trail.

Running far ahead of him, Naneh and I tried to hide. Stepping on rocks, hard caliche. Rubbing out footprints with sagebrush. Hiding behind boulders and in bushes.

We climbed trees, whispering to each other, "He won't find us. . . . He's not going to find us this time."

But it wouldn't be long before he appeared.

"I see you. . . . I see you! You're easy to find. Trailing you is like following a flock of sheep," Little Fat boasted.

We weren't good at camouflage, that was the truth. We were no challenge for him. So he moved on to other species. We helped him track deer and rabbits. Tracking coyotes was the same as dogs, we told him.

"No, no, not even," he replied.

Neither Naneh nor I cared much for this tracking business. We already knew cow cakes, horse biscuits, rabbit doo, and deer marbles, and didn't care to know more.

We always groaned and complained loudly when Little Fat wanted to play tracker..

"Do we really have to play tracker?" I demanded. "My Auntie said we shouldn't be messing around any holes, or tunnels, or dens. Something will be sure to come out and either claw us to pieces or bite us to death."

Naneh pleading, "Not all afternoon, please!"

We'd finally agree. "But only until the Sun gets to there," I'd say, measuring two hand lengths.

Naneh loudly expressed her resentment. "All we do is look for poop!"

"Yeah," I agreed. "I don't care how old and dried . . . or how steaming fresh it is. . . . I ain't touchin' it . . . not even with a stick!"

Little Fat completely disregarded what we were saying, patiently showing and telling us how similar dog . . . fox . . . coyote feces looked. Like small bullets, pointy at one end. Naneh and I paid close attention.

Then he blew it by getting far too graphic.

"There may be hair . . . and fur . . . and little bones in it."

Naneh bent over, holding her stomach. "Ohhhhhh . . . bleeeeck. . . . I'm gonna throw up. . . . I don't wanna see or hear any more about shit!"

Little Fat looked at her seriously, saying, "That word you just used . . . *shit* . . . is not the word for this. . . . This is called SKAT."

How dare he! "Little Fat," I screamed. "*Shit* is *shit*. . . . *Skat* is *shit*. It's the very same thing from the very same place. I'm going home. . . . I'm getting vomity too."

We left. He didn't care. He was scrunched over, poking around in skat!

I told my Uncle and Father about Little Fat and skat.

They were surprised he was so interested. After that they took him hunting and on fishing trips.

See . . . before Little Fat's Father left for the Spirit World, he had been a great hunter and fisherman.

So . . . Little Fat was a natural Skat Man!

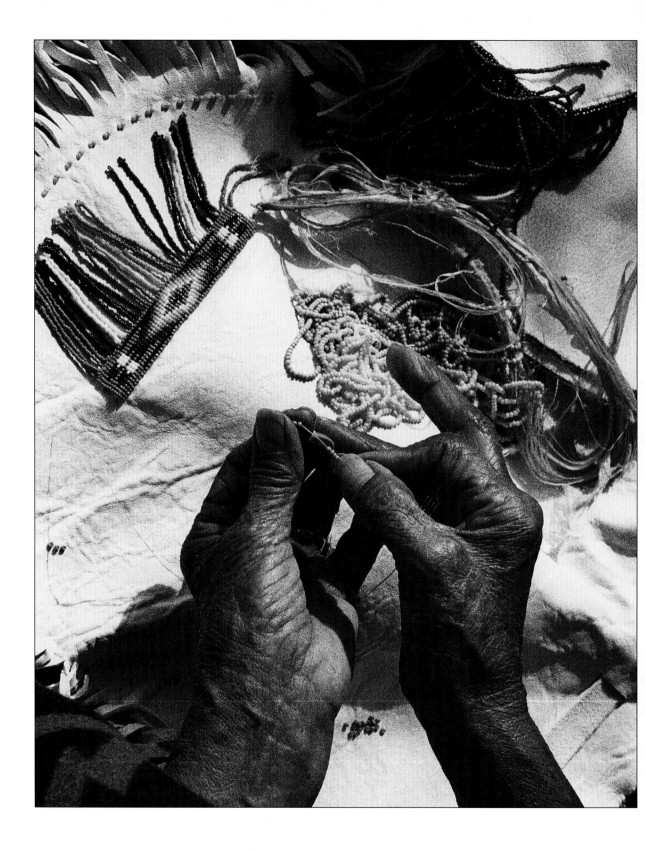

One Bead at a Time

My Grandmother and her sisters were meticulous beaders. As a very young child, I watched these women create exquisite works of art.

From fine leathers they made medicine bags, pipe bags, shirts, dresses, and moccasins onto which they beaded the intricate traditional designs of the Plains People.

My Mother took her journey to the Spirit World soon after my birth. Grandmother told me she was also a fine beader. She had made herself two full beaded buckskin dresses—one of smoked tan buckskin decorated with shells and beadwork, the other of white doeskin with a full beaded yoke. I never saw these dresses with my eyes . . . only in my mind. They were described in every detail by the Aunt for whom I'm named. She was my Mother's favorite sister. My Aunt believed that their youngest sister, who had charge of a trunk with these dresses and other family valuables, somehow lost the trunk.

In the old tribal way, my Grandmother's sisters were like honorary Grandmothers. We didn't say Grandaunts. I was taught to call them by the beloved and respectful title Grandmother.

I have memories of these women spending long days together. They brought their fine skins and beads to work on. They visited, sharing news and a meal, just happy to be together.

My Grandmother had a teepee. Behind her teepee was an arbor built by her relatives. It had a rectangular shape and was quite large, roofed and enclosed on three sides with sweet-smelling Cedar boughs. The Grandmothers always cooked out here. They took turns preparing the meal. While one cooked, the others worked on their beadwork projects.

The Grandmothers helped one another determine how best to cut the skins. Cutting leather is tricky. Some parts are hard and stiff. Other parts are stretchy and loose. Usually right down the back is even and smooth.

They beaded, using sinew for thread. I watched them strip threadlike pieces from the dried tendon, taken from the back of a cow, and draw it across the tongue. Wetting it with saliva, quickly rolling it across the knee, making a round, unbreakable thread of sinew tissue. They didn't need needles since the sinew end remained pointed as it dried.

Sharpened awls were used to make holes in the leather through which the sinew passed.

From plain leather bags, the Grandmothers removed their treasures, precious little bundles of loose beads wrapped tightly in calico cloth. They untied the bundles and carefully laid out the beads on the blankets on which they were sitting. Yes . . . they sat on blankets . . . on the ground . . . and did this perfect work! Picking up one tiny bead onto the sinew thread. Pricking holes in the skin with the sharp-pointed awl. Sewing closely together lines of beads that almost . . . by themselves . . . form beautiful designs. Some designs simple and plain. Others extravagantly bold and forceful.

One bead at a time . . .

Counting each and every bead . . .

Count . . . count . . . count . . .

Patience . . . patience . . . patience . . .

One bead at a time.

I was mesmerized by the beads. Some colors were soft and muted. The Grandmothers called these "greasy beads." Others were the imported Czechoslovakian beads with sharper, brighter colors. I thought they were all beautiful.

No one said to me, "Don't touch the beads" or seemed to worry that I'd spill them.

I touched them. Rolling them between my fingers. Fascinated by the many colors and glitter. I loved those beads, but mostly I loved watching my Grandmothers work with them. Their small wrinkled hands, deftly selecting beads. How could they laugh . . . tell stories . . . and count beads?

They were experts.

They were proficient.

They knew what they were doing!

From the hands of these women came works of unbelievable beauty.

I knew that someday . . . I would take my own place . . . beside these Grandmothers. Though not skilled as they . . . but . . . in my quest to be.

The Little Girl

My family were early risers. Up by dawn.

Auntie Elizabeth was the main cook for the Children's Dining Hall at the Boarding School. She started work at 5:30 A.M.

My Uncle Joe was Head Engineer at the Maintenance Plant. There, everything was generated for the School's upkeep. Electricity and water. Big engines pumping, ear-splitting noise all the time. You had to holler to make yourself heard in there. My Uncle was partially deaf from the engines.

My Father was one of the Indian freighters who delivered freight all over the reservations. Food supplies, all manner of furniture— office, home, school—anything that was requisitioned by the Superintendent's office.

He was always up early, loading his truck with supplies for some distant school, or traveling to the huge warehouse in Gallup, New Mexico. All shipments came by rail into Gallup, to the main warehouse. Goods were moved to smaller warehouses at Agency distribution points. From these warehouses goods were trucked out to the boarding schools and day schools.

My Father was away most of the time on freighting trips to places such as Canoncito, Ramah, Torreon, bringing back supplies for our own Crown Point Agency warehouse. Our warehouse was very large and had to be refilled constantly, as it fed many satellite schools.

I would be up before the Sun peeked over the mesas, splashing water on my face and running out to see what had taken place overnight. I'd cross the campus, then go to Auntie's for some breakfast.

One morning on approaching the small Indian Hospital, I saw an incredibly beautiful Lady up on the porch on the grey board swing, swinging slowly and brushing her long, dark hair. It fell like a thick shawl over her shoulders. As I came even with her, she looked up, giving me a slow, tender smile.

Shyly, I smiled back.

The Lady was lovely.

Thereafter, at Dawn, I would purposely cross the school campus just to look at her. And she would turn her beautiful face to me, smiling . . . wishing me a Good Morning.

Naturally I wanted to know about her. Someone said she was the wife of Chee Platero, the famous Navajo Silversmith. He had brought her from Canada; she was from the Cree Nation.

I could not get enough of the Lady's beauty. I also felt a loneliness in her person. Perhaps that was what drew me to her. For I too had a crying heart. The death of my beloved Grandmother had left me almost an orphan.

One unforgettable morning . . .

The Lady was gone . . .

The swing empty . . .

Suddenly appearing in the front door and out onto the porch was the Chief Nurse, Miss Conti. On seeing me she called, motioning me to come up onto the porch. She coolly gave me instructions to go immediately to the Employee's Kitchen, tell the cook, Lucy Brown (Little Fat's mother), to prepare this thermos, with hot, black coffee.

"Hurry, come right back. . . . Hurry!"

I ran as fast as I could to the Kitchen. Lucy Brown deftly filled the thermos, thrusting it at me, saying, "It's fresh and hot. Go!" Dashing back, I could see the hospital ambulance backed against the loading door, emitting a cloud of black fumes . . . a man sitting in the driver's seat.

No one was in the offices when I entered the Hospital. I could hear people talking in another room. Hurrying, as I was told to, I scurried toward the voices. Nurses and doctors surrounded a hospital gurney.

I was so small they didn't notice me. As they stepped back and forth doing their ministering . . . I could see . . . lying on the bed . . . a little girl . . . no bigger than I. A little girl . . . purple . . . dark bluish purple . . . unmoving . . . eyes closed.

Her dirty little clothes cast aside on the floor. Her shirt and skirts.

"That's all we can do."

"All right, get her into the ambulance."

"Call Rehoboth; let them know she's on the way."

"Too bad they waited so damn long."

One of the orderlies turned, seeing me . . .

"What are you doing in here?"

For an instant their attention was on me.

"Oh," Miss Conti said. "She's brought the coffee I sent for. Thank you. You may go now. Thank you."

Returning to what they were doing, they forgot me. I backed out, watching from the doorway as they wheeled the little girl on the gurney out into the ambulance. Two nurses jumped in. The ambulance sped away. Red lights flashing.

I was gone before the others came back in.

Outside on the porch . . . the beautiful Lady . . . still hadn't appeared.

I sat in her place . . .

Slowly swinging . . . waiting.

Maybe she will come.

Miss Conti walked out the front door, on her way to breakfast. She saw me and walked over to the swing.

"That little girl was bitten by a rattlesnake a week ago. She was out herding the family's sheep. Instead of bringing her right in, they had a medicine man treat her. He was unable to help. So finally they brought her in and expected us to fix her. It was much too late.

"Watch out for rattlesnakes," she warned.

At noon in the Dining Hall we heard that the little Navajo girl had died before reaching Rehoboth Mission.

I mourned the little girl. Thinking of her a lot.

The beautiful Lady was gone too.

Still, at Dawn I went looking for her.

After a while I stopped.

They weren't coming back.

Feast

On a rare occasion my Aunt Elizabeth would serve a great delicacy to the boarding school students: baked Prairie Dog.

My Uncle, Father, friends, and some students would stage a Prairie Dog hunt early on a Saturday morning. They'd be gone seven or eight hours, returning with plenty for a wonderful Sunday meal. These little animals are vegetarians. They live in large colonies called dog towns, really burrows underground.

As soon as the men unloaded the truck of burlap bags filled with Prairie Dogs, the assistant cooks and kitchen helpers who had been impatiently waiting would go to work, skinning, gutting, and cleaning them. Having a fine time butchering!

Naneh, Little Fat, and I watched, with Auntie telling us, "Stand back; don't get too close."

Soon there'd be a big heap of yellowish brown fur and entrails piled on a large canvas, which the big boys carried away and buried.

My Auntie orchestrated this whole performance. *"Do . . . don't . . . yes . . . no!"*

She'd have the kitchen detail wash, dry, oil, and salt the carcasses, then carefully lay them on their backs, row after row in large, heavy baking trays. These trays were put into coolers until early Sunday morning, at which time they were slid into the big ovens to bake.

The students looked forward to this meal with great anticipation.

As Sunday noon approached, Naneh, Little Fat, and I would appear at the back door to the Kitchen. Auntie on seeing us would call out,

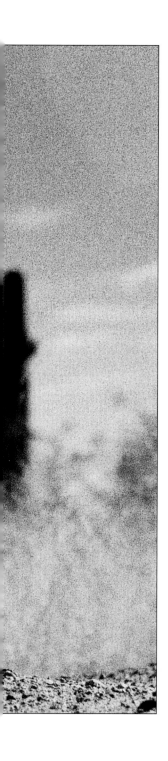

"Come in, come in. Sit over there, out of the way."

Whenever they had the Prairie Dog Feast at the Boarding School, we would come over for the festivities. It was like a big celebration of Native food. Everyone in high spirits, looking forward to this special meal.

Mr. Ance from the Bakery would make dried fruit pies for the occasion.

This was better than Thanksgiving!

The cooks bustled around, mashing potatoes, making gravy. The kitchen detail, checking things in the Dining Hall, making sure everything was in place.

Then it was time.

Tray after tray of juicy, succulent Prairie Dog came out of the big, hot ovens. Roasted to a crispy, golden brown, they looked delicious, smelling like slow-roasted chicken. Exquisite in their rows. They still had their little heads. Their little legs stuck straight up in the air.

Naneh and Little Fat left me to go eat in the Dining Hall with the students.

I appreciated this sumptuous meal.

But I just couldn't eat it.

You see, I had a pet Prairie Dog. It would have been like eating my own little pet. No, thanks!

My Auntie laughed at me, saying, "You don't know what you're missing."

And that was fine with me.

Skip Dance

We looked forward to the infrequent Skip Dances, usually held far from the Agency, requiring us to find a ride there. Generally the Indian Police would let us catch a ride with them. They had a big black van. The two officers riding in the front seat. Naneh, Little Fat, and I in the back seat, with a caged compartment for prisoners behind.

Off we'd go, dressed in our best clothes. You could smell the evening fires long before you could see the camps. Thin wisps of curling smoke. Cedar and Piñon fires.

Thanking the driver, we'd jump from the van, the policemen warning us to be ready to leave when they were or we'd be left behind. We'd visit around the large encampment, searching for the camp of our best friends . . . the Arviso family.

We'd find their camp with the wagons in a half circle, brush cedar windbreak all the way around, providing some privacy.

The Arvisos were a prominent Navajo family known all over the reservations for their fine Racehorses. The sons and daughters did the racing. All were excellent horse people.

My heart flipped on recognizing their camp. The men were standing around, talking in low voices. By the small cooking fires, the women were turning ribs and corn in husks over the coals, boiling coffee, and pulling ash bread from the low flames. We ate well.

Everyone was talking at once, happy to be together, just to see one another! I don't know which was the flashiest—the dark eyes, the white teeth, or the silver jewelry.

These nights belonged to the young and the young of heart. Suddenly the Leader began singing. The Chorus of Men followed in high-pitched, staccato voices, as only the Navajo men sing. "It's starting. . . . It's starting." Slowly we finished our meal, the Mother and the older women telling us to go on to the dance.

"Do have a good time."

"Don't be falling in love."

"Don't be coming back with a husband," they teased.

"Her . . . her, I think . . . ," they'd say, pointing with lips at which one of us they thought would be falling in love that night.

Naneh and I giggled and looked at each other.

Two bonfires. A large one for the Dancers, a smaller one for the Men's Chorus. Standing to the North, the singers were in full voice!

The Skip Dance was the one danced then. The Dancers in a big circle around their bonfire. We stood back watching, lost in the breathtaking scene before us! The older girls and women, so lovely. Velvet shirts, long swinging skirts of all colors. Hair pulled back in chongas decorated with barrettes. Stylish. Turquoise. Fringed shawls. Pendleton shawls.

By firelight it was dazzling.

When the Chorus stopped, the dance was over.

The Men's Chorus changed off and on throughout the night. Some singers taking a rest, others taking their places. When the Chorus began singing again, we nudged each other . . . stepping into the circle. The girls did the asking. You went up to a boy, tugged on his arm, and led him into the circle. Then you began dancing together, following the pair in front of you. Moving clockwise. Going in the same direction, doing the same steps.

When the singers stopped, you led your partner to the center of the circle, where he had to pay you for the dance! Usually a dime, or fifteen cents. If you were lucky—a quarter. Then you thanked him and let him go.

A little rest for the Chorus, then it begin again. Select your next partner. Collect your money!

It was much fun. If a boy danced and had no money or, worse, wouldn't pay, you could take his hat . . . bracelet . . . anything loose. Your friends would come to help you collect. They just stood around him. He would be so embarrassed because of the awful attention, he'd finally give something.

You didn't just dance with people you knew. You could select strangers. Anybody. People were there for a good time. Even though we were young, it was proper if we asked an old man to dance. He still had to go to the center of the circle and pay.

Surrounding the circle were older people, sitting, visiting, watching. Like chaperons.

When we got tired, we'd go back to camp, drink coffee, take a little break, then go back to the circle. The older girls danced with shawls draped around their shoulders. If a girl liked a boy, they'd both be wrapped in her shawl.

"Like tamales," we said, and chuckled as they danced by us. "Real hot tamales."

Not us. We didn't even own shawls. If we had, we'd never let a boy under them!

Toward early morning we'd be danced out, bidding our friends good-bye. Glad to be catching our ride home.

The Men's Chorus, a hundred men or more, sang on.

Greeting Dawn Boy. Little Chief.

If in a few days you were to return to this place, you would still hear the Men's Chorus singing.

High . . . shrill . . . unforgettable.

The mesas and canyons holding the very essence of their voices. Reluctant to give them up.

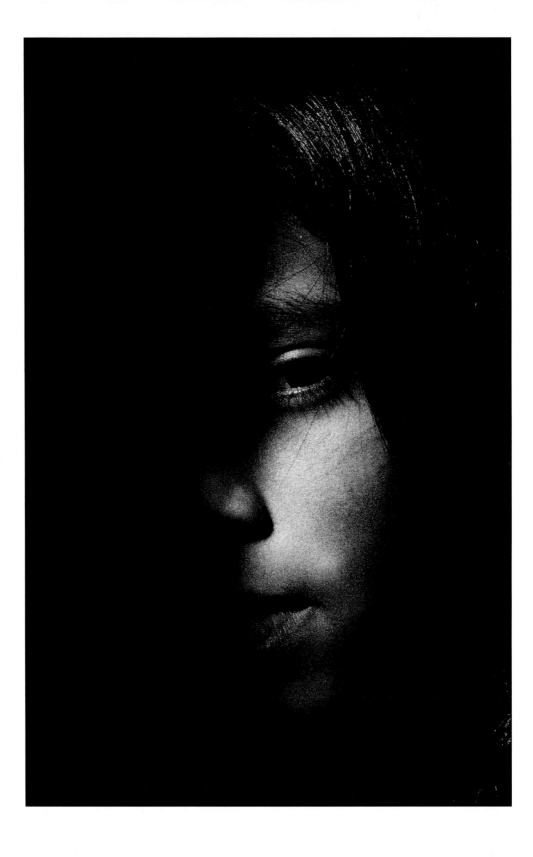

Testimonial

Fact: Nine young Navajo boys ages twelve to thirteen ran away from the Crown Point Indian School in late April just before school was over for the year.

Fact: They hid in the mesas far, far beyond the Hawk's Eye.

Fact: They stole a Goat from the school's goatherd. They butchered, roasted, and ate it.

Fact: They were tracked down, returned, and thrown in the Jailhouse.

Fact: The following day a special assembly was called for all students in the third to sixth grades by Mr. Durham, the Boys' Disciplinarian. In the Boarding School Auditorium.

On the afternoon of the assembly, I was down at the one-room day school. We were practicing a little program for the end-of-year activities, to be held in two weeks at the Boarding School.

My teacher, Miss Bonnie, sent me to get the keys so she could take her students for rehearsal in the Boarding School Auditorium, where all events were held.

Skipping along . . . I was happy to be running this errand for Miss Bonnie. From the bright sunshine, I entered the large, darkened hall of the school, which led directly into the Auditorium.

I could hear a man's loud, excited, angry voice rising in fury.

It was the first time I'd ever heard anything like this. . . . I stopped . . . midway in the hall . . . listening. Strangely no one was around. It seemed the building was empty, except for the violent voice raging on like a crazed animal.

The voice was coming from the Auditorium.

Silently . . . I inched toward it. The big, swinging doors to the Auditorium were closed. Usually these doors were opened during assemblies. Not today. The doors did not close together. There was a half-inch crack from top to bottom.

Stealthily . . . holding my breath . . . I looked through the crack. I saw the nine boys on the stage and Mr. Durham in an evil rage. He was beating the boys with a horsewhip. Shouting obscenities about running away . . . about goats . . . about rules . . . about disobeying.

I was transfixed.

The boys never screamed. They were moaning, falling, as the whip delivered blows. *Hnh . . . Hnh.* Across their shoulders, backs, buttocks. There was blood . . . lots of it.

I didn't want to see this. But . . .

I couldn't move.

I was paralyzed.

I couldn't breathe.

My throat had closed.

I too was dying.

The whip . . . cracking before my eyes.

Finally it stopped. . . .

The boys lying or half sitting, dazed, in disbelief.

Mr. Durham strode to the center of the stage. Shaking his whip in the air, he seemed exhausted, but his voice boomed out to the students in the audience. "Let this be an example to all of you of what to expect if there are any more runaways or thieving."

With that he jumped from the stage and strode down the aisle toward the big, swinging doors. Eyes fixed straight ahead.

Feebly I crept under the stairs, where the oil mops were stored. I heard his heavy breathing as he passed. The main door slammed shut. The students—mute, expressionless—filed out, emptying the building.

When finally I could move, I came out from under the stairs. I entered the Auditorium.

The atmosphere was like death had just happened there.

I smelled the blood.

I smelled the fear, or . . . was it mine?

Stunned, I took a seat. Gradually my senses returned.

I heard noises . . . like babies' muffled cries. I got to my feet and walked very slowly up the aisle toward the stage. The cries were now audible. They came from outdoors, on the west side. I saw a fire exit door slightly ajar. Peering out, I saw the brutally beaten boys lying half-conscious against the building. Barely comprehending what had happened to them. I saw, hurrying to their assistance, the Indian dormitory matrons and helpers.

Softly, softly, I closed the door.

Turning to leave, I noticed the stage floor aglitter. Looking closely, I saw bright, shiny seed beads scattered everywhere. The cruel whip had cut into the beautiful beaded belts the boys wore, destroying them.

Terrified, expecting a whip lashing across my own thin shoulders, I slipped quickly from the empty building. What I had witnessed that late Spring afternoon haunted me. I carried a mortal shame, fear, and hurt away with me.

Fact: I was just eight years old.

Phoenix
Indian School

Valley of the Sun

It was time to begin my journey. A journey that would take me into another life, a life no one can conceive of unless he or she has lived it.

Native American children were taken from their homes. Others, such as me, were sent by consent of parents who knew that unless they conformed to the law that all Indian children be sent to United States Indian Schools, the children would be taken forcibly.

Aunt Elizabeth: "We were seized and taken as captives."

Uncle Joe: "We were stolen away."

My Father: "Kidnapped."

Sitting in shadows, trying to be invisible, I listened to my elders' horrifying stories of when they were sent away. I did not see them as they were—sitting there talking as old people. I saw them as small children terrified of the strangers who came to tear them from their mothers' arms. Mothers who pleaded, "Don't take my child. . . . Please . . . don't take my child. . . . My child's too little to be taken away. . . . He can't speak your language. . . . He'll die. . . . We don't know the White Man's way. . . . You're going to kill him!"

Uncle Joe recalling what his Mother and Father told him about the time they almost died from worry and walked ninety miles to the Indian Boarding School to see if he was still alive. It took them three and a half days. They didn't speak any English and couldn't make themselves understood.

Going from building to building, looking for their child. The bigger children told them the White Building was where the smaller boys were.

They went to the White Building and tried to talk to the White Matron who didn't understand who they wanted to see. Finally she took them out to the back of the building. There were about fifteen little boys sitting on the ground, some leaning against the building . . . crying . . . moaning . . . *Unnnnnn . . . Unnnnnn.*

The parents looked and looked at the children but couldn't recognize their son. *He's not here. . . . They killed him!* they thought. The little boys' heads were shaven, and all were wearing baggy blue coveralls and big black shoes. They all looked alike. At last their son saw them, jumped up, and rushed to his parents. But before he reached them, he stopped, embarrassed by the oversized blue coveralls, the laced high-top shoes so big they rubbed blisters, and worst of all . . . his shaved head.

My Uncle never forgot how waves of shame flooded over him . . . again and again . . . because of how bad he must have looked to his parents.

"My Mother . . . My Father."

In shock and disbelief the parents drew their only child close against their bodies . . . turning from the other children . . . to hide their faces.

And so their stories went, each telling of fear . . . shame . . . subjugation. With government officials, the missionaries, and the police to enforce the law, the majority of Indian parents dutifully sent their children away.

My own Mother went to Chilacco Indian School in Oklahoma. My Father to Phoenix Indian School in Arizona, where I was destined.

—⁓⁓—

Since arriving at Crown Point I had grown close to Aunt Elizabeth, who was devoted to Uncle Joe and to her work. For me she was the warm, caring, strong one.

Uncle Joe was nearly deaf . . . a stern, quiet man. Neither he nor I needed many words. It was he who patiently taught me to shoot, hunt, and fish. I learned to shoot with a crazy little .22 rifle whose sight was gone. But never mind . . . I didn't need it!

My Father was no father. He didn't have the faintest idea how to be one. He grew up in Indian School under the strictest of military regimes and never got over it. Knowing this, the relatives on my mother's side of the family had begged him to leave me with them.

He said no.

Aunt Elizabeth and Uncle Joe asked him to let them take me as their own child.

He said no.

A wealthy, childless missionary couple, Dr. and Mrs. Bolt, of the Dutch Reformed Church asked my Father to allow them to raise me.

He said no.

My Father had decided he knew what was best for me. He had decided I would go to Phoenix Indian School as he had.

~~~~

Summer was over and it was time for me to leave for Boarding School. On the last day, Naneh, Little Fat, and I sat high atop our favorite mesa, the Rattlesnake. I told my friends of my apprehensions . . . sobbing . . . telling them how frightened I was to be leaving.

Again, the unknown place.

Again, among strangers.

I was full of fear and tears.

On that last evening in Crown Point, Aunt Elizabeth held me close, whispering, "You'll be back in nine months."

Nine months? She could've said nine years. It sounded like forever.

Uncle Joe, in his soft, broken English, said, "All Innin chilrens gotta do this. We did it. You coming back. . . . We going fishing . . . Bluewater." Motioning toward the East with pursed lips, "Bluewater."

Early in the morning my Father called out to me. It was time to get up. I prepared quickly so as not to keep him waiting. He was warming up his truck.

When I stepped outside, Naneh and Little Fat were waiting. Surprising me.

My Father said, "Get in . . . time to go."

Naneh, Little Fat, and I just looked at one another.

Saying good-bye with our eyes.

I climbed into the truck.

With whining gears, we pulled away.

My friends and I . . . still looking our good-byes.

—ɯɯ—

In Gallup, New Mexico, we went to the Train Depot. My Father had breakfast in the Harvey House. I couldn't eat.

Finally the train arrived. *Shewwww . . . shewwww.* Expelling great puffs of steam clouds, halfway covering the engine. Everything seemed to shake. Standing on the redbrick walk, we waited.

Before the train had completely stopped, a tall, elegant conductor came gracefully down the steps. He was a black man, wearing a dark blue uniform.

My Father awkwardly kissed my forehead. Squirming, I wished he hadn't. I didn't want his ol' kiss. He was sending me away. No kiss from me, that was for sure!

He asked the Black Conductor to take good care of me to Phoenix. Glancing at the ticket, the Black Conductor said, "She'll have to change trains in Ashfork. We don't go south to Phoenix. We go straight west to California."

Ohhhhhhh . . . This sounded very bad. Change trains? What if it's the wrong train? . . . What'll I do?

"All aboard."

Stepping on a little box, I scooted up. I watched the Black Conductor as he picked up the little box and swung himself up the steps. Following him into the train, he showed me where to sit.

"Here, you can have this whole seat to yourself. Nobody to bother you." My anxiety and distress apparent to him, he comforted me. "Everything's going to be fine. . . . Don't worry. . . . You'll see."

The train slowly left the station. *Chug . . . chug . . . chug.* The whistle blasting out a warning. *Woo . . . woo . . . woo . . . woo.*

Looking out the window.

Hot tears flooding my face.

In the distance I saw my Father walking away.

I wasn't crying for him.

I was crying for me.

The Black Conductor returned with a pillow and blanket, saying, "Take a little nap if you want to or just watch out the window. We'll see the Painted Desert soon. Ever been there? Watch for it. It's something to see! I'll bet you haven't eaten. . . . Have you?"

"I can't eat," I told him.

"Well now, let me tell you something. We've got some good food cooking back there. Pretty soon I'll bring you some. Maybe you'll try . . . hmmmmm . . . just a little bit . . . hmmmmm?"

He brought the food. I devoured it, then fell asleep, missing the Painted Desert!

In Ashfork we left his train, taking my little cardboard suitcase and a brown paper sack he'd packed with food. He took me into the small Train Station, giving my ticket to the bored Station Clerk. The Clerk said, "The train for Phoenix will be here in an hour. I'll see that she gets on all right."

The Black Conductor walked out of the station. I followed him. He turned, stooping down . . . holding my shoulders . . . speaking softly . . . looking in my eyes, once more saying, "Everything's going to be fine. . . . Don't worry. . . . You'll see."

He knew my heart was breaking from yesterday's sorrows and tomorrow's fears.

I didn't want him to leave me. I wanted to go to California with him. As the train for California left, he waved to me from the vestibule of his car. I waved until his train was a teeny speck, wishing I could've stayed on that train forever.

Sitting in a slippery wooden seat in the small Station of Ashfork, Arizona, I opened the brown paper sack and ate the food the Black Conductor had given me. I was the only passenger around.

Before long the Clerk called to me, "The train to Phoenix is almost due." I asked if he was sure it was the train to Phoenix. He replied very seriously, "Oh yes, only one train goes south in the afternoon. It's the Phoenix-El Paso train. Due in there at 7:00 P.M. You're going to the Valley of the Sun. Did you know that? It gets pretty warm down in the Valley. It's a garden place. You're going to like it."

Oh yeah . . . I'm gonna hate it. . . . I hate it already . . . so just shut up . . . shut up . . . shut up. That little uncontrollable voice in my head.

—

Clickety . . . clickety . . . clickety . . . clickety. We puffed into the Grand Phoenix Train Station.

Lightning bolts were jagging all over the sky. Deafening claps of thunder rolled on and on and on. Rain was blasting down.

Valley of the Sun . . . huh?

Fierce winds were tormenting the tall palm trees. Bending them like cornstalks.

Swooshing palm fronds.
Beating one another
As if to release themselves
As if to be gone, into this
Wild terrifying Night.

Pausing . . . hesitantly . . . I came down the steps off the train into the arms of Marie E. Bebout. She gathered me up . . . hugging . . . hugging some more . . . tears glistening in her eyes . . . softly . . . softly . . . saying over and over . . .

> *Esther's child*
> *Esther's child*
> *Esther's child*

You see . . . Esther was my Mother's given Christian name.

She and Marie E. Bebout were classmates and the closest of friends through all their years together at Chilacco Indian School in Oklahoma.

Everything's going to be fine. . . . Don't worry. . . . You'll see!

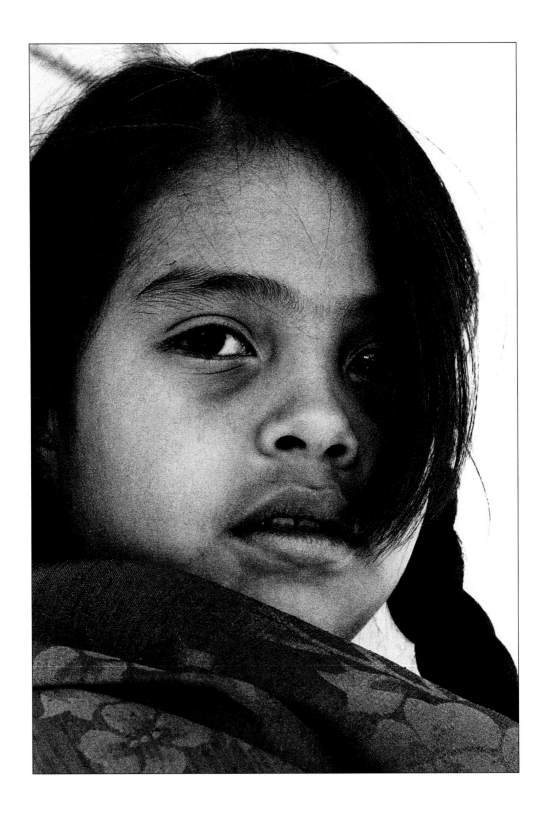

Killing the Indian

On that first day I met other children who had just arrived and, like me, didn't know what to expect. We found out very soon. The first order of business was to make sure all the children were healthy. That meant an inspection of the entire body.

The delousing and body scrub-down were very important! A skin infection called impetigo was especially dreaded, as were lice. Should we have head lice . . . or sores . . . it would spread quickly to the other children.

First they fine-combed our hair. If someone had lice she was immediately given the kerosene treatment and her hair was cut very, very short!

After the delousing . . . the scrub-down!

The big girls took us into the steamy Shower Room and told us to undress and get in the shower stall.

Taking off my clothes as quickly as possible . . . throwing them on a small bench . . . I jumped in the stall . . . pulling shut the duck cloth curtain . . . not wanting anyone looking at my nakedness.

Inside, I just stood there not knowing how to manipulate the knobs that controlled the water.

A Big Girl threw aside the shower curtain for the whole world to see me naked! Turning on the water she said, "We have to do this. . . . If it's too hot say so."

It was too hot . . . and I said so! It mattered not. She had the power to do with me what she would . . . and I couldn't tell on her.

In the soap tray above the knobs was a bar of Government Issue Brown Soap, GIBS it was called, and a hard-bristled eight-inch-by-three-inch scrub brush. The Big Girl rubbed the laundry soap onto the brush . . . grabbed me . . . and proceeded to skin me ALIVE!

Oh-h-h-h-h . . . my poor, tender little body. Other girls began scream-ing . . . but the surprise of this torture left me voiceless. I wanted to fall down and die! Only . . . the Big Girl was holding me up. Finally she said, "Rinse and dry off. Wrap the towel around yourself and go to the Clothing Room."

In the large Clothing Room we were issued clothes. The new girls were put in a line-up according to size. The smallest, such as me, were sent to Company K . . . the littlest girls' company. Company K had four squads . . . six children to a squad. Other girls' companies . . . from A to J . . . had eight squads, eight girls to a squad. All companies had a cap-tain, two lieutenants, and two or more sergeants.

Now I belonged to a company and a squad. In my squad were three other eight-year-olds: Eunice, Eva, and Christine. We four quickly drew together.

Company K Captain Nona Kay was of the Hopi tribe . . . very short and nearly square with a high, piping voice. First Lieutenant Mary Ann Polacca was also Hopi, and Second Lieutenant Wimmie Tall Man was Navajo.

For a while it was confusing, but in a short time we understood how to "Fall In" and be accounted for. Each child had her own place "In Line." If someone was absent, it created a gap in the line. That person was immediately reported missing and a search party sent out.

Thus began our strict military training under the Bureau of Indian Affairs. All emphasis was on work, drilling, and marching; discipline, behavior, and correctness.

In the morning at 0600, military time for 6:00 A.M., the bugles blew and the big gongs sounded throughout the buildings. We jumped up, making our beds immediately. Then we hurried down the stairs to dress . . . wash our faces . . . brush our teeth . . . comb our hair . . .

straighten our lockers . . . all before the next gong sounded. At 0630 it was time to "Fall In" for half an hour of drilling.

"*Company . . . atten . . . tion!*" Nona Kay piped. We stood ramrod straight . . . arms at our sides . . . with our little feet at right angles to each other.

"*Company . . . right . . . face!*" Nona Kay piped again. This meant we were to turn our heads to the right and look over our right shoulders. Not quite. She demonstrated how it was done. She stood before us snapping her head.

"*Right . . . face!*". . . Snap.

"*Left . . . face!*". . . Snap.

We got it! She nearly had us snapping our heads off!

The bugles blew. It was 0700—time for breakfast.

Nona instructed us, "On my word . . . *March!* You step off on your LEFT foot."

"*Forward . . . march!*"

Staggering and stumbling we tried to get off on the right foot. It was a pathetic, irregular line to the Dining Hall. Company K was the last to enter the Dining Hall. I was amazed. . . . Everyone else was still standing when we arrived. That was the procedure.

Your squad was assigned a table. Each child had a particular seat at the table. For the rest of the school year this was where you took your meals. We stood behind our chairs until Grace was said, then sat down to eat. It was extremely orderly.

That first meal had another surprise for me. The Boys' Disciplinarian stepped up onto the stage, at the front of the hall. . . . I could hardly believe my eyes . . . It was Mr. Durham! The Boys' Disciplinarian from Crown Point . . . the one who beat the hell out of the Navajo boys with the horsewhip!

We little kids sat to the far side of the Hall, which was good. Mr.

Durham wouldn't see me. I was so afraid of him. I watched him leading the prayer . . . blessing our food . . . looking so pious.

How did HE get here . . . from the tiny boarding school in New Mexico to this immense school in Arizona? It was a big promotion for him. But not for long. After a couple of months he was transferred again . . . to a small boarding school in Tuba City, Arizona. Bad employees were never fired. The Bureau of Indian Affairs merely transferred them.

And so . . . each morning a bit more was learned. New orders . . . such as . . .

"No slouching!"

"Heads . . . up!"

"Shoulders . . . back!"

"Eyes . . . straight ahead!"

"Forward . . . march!"

"Your left . . . your left . . . your left two, three, four . . . your left . . ."

"Company . . . halt!"

"Dress right. . . . Dress!"

Your head turned right . . . your left hand was placed smartly on your hip . . . elbow extended. This order gave you twelve inches from the person on either side . . . so you weren't jammed up against one another.

"Move down. . . . Move down!" the lieutenants barked. "Give each other enough space." Showing us how to "dress" our arms.

"Right . . . face!" squeaked our captain. Half of us turned our faces right. Others turned their whole bodies left.

"Raise your right hands. . . . Do you know your right hand from your left? When I give you an order . . . *Right face!* you will . . . turn to your right. . . . You will . . . pivot on your right heel . . . like this!" Turning her little fat self a smart ninety degrees to the right our captain said, "See . . . easy. Now let's get it right!"

"Right . . . face!"

A lot of awkward bumping and unsteadiness.

"*Left . . . face!*"

She fooled us! We thought we were going to keep turning right. Trying to stay on our feet . . . then another order.

"*About . . . face!*"

"Ladies! Like this!" She placed her right foot smartly behind her left foot . . . toe to heel . . . and spun around 180 degrees and snapped back into "Attention" position. Oh, what a fine little top she was!

We began to understand this new way of walking and carrying ourselves. Executing the commands as quickly as they were given was a true discipline for the mind and body. And . . . we did get it!

Bugle Calls

At Phoenix Boarding School the buglers kept our lives moving in strict military order. The bugles called us for classes, work, lunch, supper, any evening activities.

They said these bugle calls played an important part in the Civil War. They were the very calls used by buglers of the United States Cavalry and the United States Army when they chased our grandparents across the plains, mountains, swamps, and deserts . . . on the long walks . . . in the forts of Laramie, Kearny, and Defiance.

Now decades later, little Indian children's lives were dictated by these same bugle calls.

At 0600 we awakened to the bugle blowing on the far side of the school campus. Arise.

The buglers blew at 0700 for breakfast formation and raising of the American flag. The flag was slowly raised up a tall flagpole while all students saluted even if you weren't anywhere near the flagpole. We little girls stood at attention, saluting, two blocks away.

Assembly, which we knew as "Last Call," was played throughout the day. It called us to formations and any other time we were to assemble. It was fast . . . frenetic. . . . It meant business. Last call . . . no more warnings . . . this was it. Late to "Last Call" . . . DEMERITS. We moved quickly as it intended us to. Assemble!

Somewhere this "Last Call" was given words:

> *There's a monkey*
> *In the grass*
> *With his finger*

Up his ass
Pull it out
Pull it out
Pull it out

We wondered, what young soldier made up this foul wording? Where was he . . . what war? And how did it reach us? Bugler to bugler to bugler? The origin of these naughty lyrics was a mystery, but we all knew these words by heart. We sang them at the top of our lungs when the matrons and officers were not around.

The last of the bugle calls was blown at night.
2200 . . . 10:00 P.M. Taps.
There was a great transformation here. The bustling, noisy school settled down to rest. A complete silence fell across the entire campus.
Up in our second-floor, open-screened Dormitory, we snuggled in and listened, a soft scent of orange blossoms wafting in on pure air.
From a distance the buglers sweetly and softly blew their last message of the day. That most hauntingly beautiful of all bugle calls. Taps.

Go to sleep
Go to sleep
Sleep and rest
All is well
God is nigh
Go to sleep
Go to sleep
Go to sleep

Inspections

Now, let it be told about the endless inspections. It seemed that every day there was an inspection of some kind. For instance . . .

FINGERNAIL INSPECTION:

At any formation, if there were two extra minutes . . . fingernails.

Dutifully we held out our hands, palms down. The officers examined each squad's hands.

"Dirty . . . dir . . . ty . . . fin . . . ger . . . nails. Germs!"

On to the next child . . . "Too long . . . cut those nails. Are you trying to be a wild animal?"

All eyes shifting to the wild animal.

The Officer traveled down the line, whapping her pointer finger across our little fingers. *Whap . . . whap . . . whap!*

"Chewing your nails, huh? Better stop or they'll scratch the inside of your stomach."

HEAD INSPECTION:

Weekly.

Pray nothing's crawling around in your hair . . . living on your head . . . because the Kerosene Squad was geared for immediate action!

EAR INSPECTION:

The Officer scrutinized each ear in great detail.

"There's something growing in all that old yellow wax."

The first time I was told this I imagined vines growing to my shoulders. I begged Eva to look in my ears and tell me what she saw.

She peered into one and then the other.

"Nothing . . . *nada*. Those old snots, they always say that. Why don't they just say, 'Wash your ears.' Snots!"

SHOE INSPECTION:

At any lineup shoes were given a swift inspection.

Each child was issued a small shoe brush and a can of black paste. You brushed your shoes every day.

Apply black shoe paste.

Let dry.

Buff until you get a high shine.

LOCKER INSPECTION:

All our clothing was tagged with our assigned numbers, issued to each child when she entered school. We kept those numbers until we left the Little Girls' Building. Mine was eighty-four. Small white tags, with our numbers, were sewn inside the top of each stocking. Shoes were marked with indelible marking on the insides.

In your locker your two dresses and sweater had to be hung three inches apart, to ventilate. Your second pair of shoes and your slippers on the bottom shelf neatly placed side by side. Toilet articles—toothbrush, tooth powder, comb, and bar of soap—belonged in a row on the top shelf. Towel and washcloth had to be hung, just so, on a little bar inside the locker door.

Everything had its place. Everything better be *in* its place. Demerits when you failed locker inspection.

BLOOMER INSPECTION:

We wore bloomers. Real bloomers made by the big girls in their Home Economics classes. They were constructed of unbleached muslin—with full bottom cut to the knee. They puffed out a little or a lot, depending on the size of your rear end. The snug elastic around the knee kept them from falling down, also making them blouse out. I looked like a big pumpkin in my bloomers!

Miss Saylor, the Girls' Adviser, was convinced girls wouldn't wear bloomers if they could get away with it. She was the Bloomer Patrol . . . the Bloomer Inspector . . . the Bloomer Commissar!

Miss Saylor would sneak behind us and yank up our dresses to see if we were wearing our bloomers, and wearing them correctly—down to the knee! If your bloomers were not to the knee, five demerits—an hour labor for each demerit.

You never knew when she'd ambush you and jerk up your dress to see your bloomers. It didn't matter where you were either . . . on your way to school, work detail, or just any place, any time. When Miss Saylor felt the urge to look at bloomers, she looked!

None of the other matrons or assistants did this. They didn't care to see our bloomers. Only Miss Saylor wanted to look! It was really embarrassing. I hated it. Whoaaaaa . . . there she is . . . up my dress . . . again!

Miss Saylor was top heavy. Her breasts took up the whole upper front of her body. She was skinny-assed and -legged. She wore pointy shoes with three-inch heels that threw her forward. With that abundant top, she walked tilted, swishing her arms across her butt to keep herself upright.

"Like a chimpanzee," we said, imitating her walk.

Hunch forward . . . step . . . *swish* . . . step . . . *swish* . . . step . . . *swish*.

Pretending to jerk up dresses!
No . . . no . . . it wasn't nice. We knew this.
In our humiliation we wanted to scream . . . to shriek!
But we learned early—laughing was best.

The Work Details

Running as large an institution as our school entailed many jobs. The little girls' schedule included:

The Laundry Detail
The Dining Room Detail
The Sewing Detail
The schedules changed every six weeks.

Some work details were in the morning from 8:00 A.M. to 11:30 A.M. Then we'd go to classes in the afternoon from 1:00 P.M. to 4:00 P.M. As details shifted, we'd reverse our schooltime to mornings and work afternoons. You always knew where you had to be as schedules were posted on all the bulletin boards.

If you didn't understand where you were supposed to be, there were always the officers who took you to the bulletin board and made sure you learned to read and understand how these schedules operated. They were coordinated to mesh and fit effectively. They worked well.

―――

I did not care for the Laundry Detail and was happy when those six weeks were up.

The Laundress, Miss Lettie Bowman, was a tall, reed-thin person. She wore ankle-length dresses with long sleeves and chin-high collars closed tightly with a brooch. She pulled her hair straight back in a knot, a white dimity cap anchoring it. She had huge, brown eyes that looked out coldly from magnified horn-rimmed glasses. We called her The Pilgrim.

The Assistant Laundress was Miss Louise, a small, petite woman, young and pretty. She was from the Pima tribe of Arizona. We learned our duties from her.

The Pilgrim never smiled, never spoke to us. Even if we children were standing right in front of her. She'd motion Miss Louise over to tell her what it was she wanted us to do, all the time giving us that cold stare.

Marcus Whitman was in charge of all the machinery in the Laundry. I don't know what his title was. I do know he was the one who really ran the Laundry. He was a strong young man from the Papago tribe of Arizona. He was the person who kept the big commercial washing machines, the dryers, the tumblers, and the mangles running. If anything broke down, he repaired it.

The Laundry was a long rectangular building. Two thirds of it housed the machines for washing. The other third was called the Ironing Room. Long, narrow ironing boards extended out from the walls, and the bigger girls stood there for hours—hand-ironing dresses, shirts, skirts, and pants. The Pilgrim's desk was in this room. She was usually sitting at her desk.

In this same ironing department were two ugly machines called pressers. I was afraid of them. The girls working these pressers had to concentrate on what they were doing. Otherwise they might scorch the item they were pressing . . . God forbid! But worse than that, they could get horribly burned on their hands or arms. Every so often, someone was rushed to the hospital for burn treatment. I hated those pressers. Even the noise they made sounded mean and dangerous. They hissed . . . *Shcooooooooo . . . schooooooooo.*

The Laundry Room where we little girls worked was hot and steamy. It depended on the weather if the doors and windows were opened. The Laundry Detail usually had ten or twelve children. The soiled laundry was sorted in the dormitories before being transferred to the Laundry, where it was placed in five-foot-by-five-foot wheeled carts. Whatever was delivered to the Laundry before 8:00 A.M. was returned washed, pressed, and folded to the department it came from by 5:00 P.M. the same day.

Mr. Whitman and his helpers had charge of washing, rinsing, and drying the clothes. The big machines thumped and groaned, spewing suds and water onto the floor. Six-inch-wide gutters carried the excess suds and water down heavy, iron-webbed drains.

The little girls' duty was to take care of the flatwork—sheets, pillowcases, tablecloths, napkins, and the like. The commercial-sized mangle, a huge machine with barrel-like pressers, was kept rolling for this flatwork most of the time.

Two girls were required to send a sheet through the mangle. First, each girl picked up the damp sheet by the seamed top or bottom. Then one girl at each end of the sheet stretched it full width and sent it into the hot, cushioned mangle. Two girls on the opposite side of the mangle caught the ends of the sheet as it fell onto a long table, moving aside so that two other girls could catch the next sheet, and so on. You folded your sheet in half lengthwise, then half again. Finally each sheet was folded down to a square about fourteen inches by fourteen inches.

When doing pillowcases or napkins, three or four girls would send them through the mangle at once. That many girls on the other side caught and stacked them neatly to be later folded in half, half again, and half once more.

The Laundry Detail was hard for children. There was no place to sit down. The floors were concrete, and our legs tired quickly. Sometimes if we got tired enough, we'd take a little break. Plopping into one of the carts on top of dirty linen to take a little snooze!

The employees, immersed in their deadlines, wouldn't miss a little girl or two for a while. If it appeared you were being missed, another girl would hurl a wet knotted towel at you. You'd climb out of the cart and saunter back to where you were supposed to be.

At 9:30 A.M. we were given a ten-minute recess, not one second over. We'd go outside to play for those ten minutes.

Then poking her head out the door, The Pilgrim would tap her little desk bell . . . *Ding . . . ding . . . ding . . .* and we'd file back in to work.

At 11:30 A.M. the work whistle blew, releasing us to return to our Dormitory.

For me it wasn't so much the chores that I disliked at the Laundry, it was the loud, incessant noise of the machines. For others it was the specks of lint floating, nearly invisible, through the air . . . causing watery eyes and endless sneezing.

But even in this horrible place, romance bloomed.

We watched Miss Louise and Mr. Whitman exchange long, sweet looks across the endless mountains of sheets. They fell in love . . . and got married.

We still called her Miss Louise.

As for The Pilgrim, Miss Bowman, I felt she needed my Auntie's kind teachings . . . that a hello . . . a nod . . . a smile . . . were simple and valuable courtesies.

For myself, I learned to assume an air of total indifference toward her, The Pilgrim.

The Dining Room Detail was different from the other work shifts because of the time requirement. It began at 6:30 A.M.

The cooks, having already prepared the meal, awaited the arrival of the detail to put the food on the tables. We had to work quickly as the student body arrived for breakfast at 7:00 A.M.

Two children were responsible for setting up and clearing six tables. You and a partner were assigned these six tables, and they were your responsibility for the length of your detail.

We pushed metal carts to the huge kitchen windows where the cooks put out big pitchers of milk or cocoa. Large, oval pewter dishes of oatmeal or Cream of Wheat, always some kind of gravy. At the bakery window we picked up platters of fresh sliced bread. From the metal cart we transferred this food to the tables.

We did not plunk dishes down helter-skelter on the tables. No, each container had its own place. The bread platter here. . . . The cereal bowl there. . . . Honey . . . butter . . . two sets of salt and pepper in the center of the table.

We'd barely finish setting the food on the tables before the student body arrived. Taking our place at our own table, standing behind our chairs, we were eight to a table at assigned seats. Two officers presided at all meals—one at each end of the table with three children on either side. We stood as the Boys' Disciplinarian stepped up onto the little stage to make announcements concerning the student body. Then he led us in this spoken prayer . . .

Thou art great and thou art good
And we thank thee for this food
By His hand we all are fed
Thank you, Lord, for our daily bread.

We ate in silence, except for a murmured request for more of this or that, always prefaced by "Please."

"Please may I have . . ."

"Please pass . . ."

Nothing accepted without a "Thank You."

The big girls smiled and nodded approval. The dining hall assistants roamed about making sure everything was fine. As the meal ended, we passed our plates, bowls, cups, and silverware to the ends of the table to be stacked. This procedure, taking only seconds, was nearly as important as eating the meal.

Then, on signal, the students rose and filed out of the Dining Room in an orderly fashion. We, the detail, remained.

In the aisles, we piled the chairs one on top of the other, upside down. Again we pulled those carts table to table, loading them with dirty dishes.

Then on to the Dishwashing Room. Here were the long tunnels of commercial dishwashing machines. The bigger girls took over our carts, loading the plates, bowls, and so forth into the dishwasher trays that then rolled through the blistering hot, soapy water and into the scalding rinses. The dishes came out dry from the heat. Only the silverware was dried by hand—to eliminate water spots.

As our dishes were being washed, we little girls wiped the tables clean. The floors were also swept and mopped after every meal. With that finished, it was back to the Dishwashing Room for our carts, now loaded with hot, sanitized dishes and flatware.

Quickly, we set up the tables. It was easy. All tables were set in exactly the same order . . . plates face down . . . knife and teaspoon to the right of the plate . . . fork over napkin on the left. Cups and glasses also had their places, as did the tall pitchers.

We scurried back and forth, vying to be the first ones done with our tables. When we finished, we'd help some slowpokey girls with their work . . . all the while chiding them for being lazy, not fast like us!

Everyone had to be finished with her assignments before any of us could leave. We always traveled in a group. Waiting while the dining assistants inspected our tables, we'd sit up on the little stage viewing the rows and rows of tables now set with clean, softly gleaming pewter dishes.

Looking across that now spotless Dining Room gave us a good feeling. Everything was properly and efficiently completed . . . and each of us had a thorough part in this important detail!

—————

The second floor of the Domestic Arts Building was the domain of Miss Jensen, head of the Sewing Detail. She was a strict-faced woman who had been teaching Indian children to sew for probably one hundred years.

Very regal, her body was held up in place by a tight corset. This apparatus seemed to hinder her movements. She walked slowly, every step deliberate. Around her neck, on a long gold chain, dangled a large key.

When she sat at her desk, so straight, so stiff, I thought of her as a rocket—ready to blast out of its casing!

To her face, we called her Miss Jensen. Behind her back . . . Thimbles. During our classes she wore two thimbles, one on her forefinger, another on her middle finger. These were her weapons of choice.

She began our instruction in a large room called the Cutting Room,

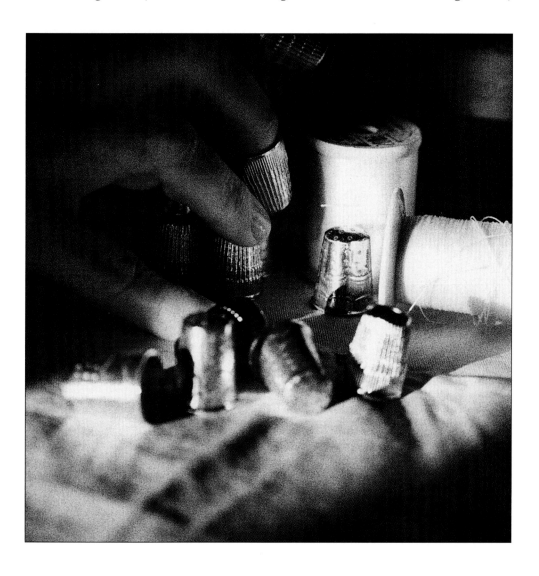

with long tables and stationary ironing boards. Our first weeks in the Cutting Room were devoted to one-quarter-inch seams. Miss Jensen said, "When you learn to make seams, *then* we'll go to the Sewing Room."

On practice material we measured again and again, one-quarter-inch seams. We'd mark faint pencil marks at exactly one-quarter inch of material, which was then turned under, creating the seam. Then she taught us to thread a needle, to baste down the seam.

When that was perfected, we learned to use the iron. It mattered not if we burned ourselves. . . . "Just DON'T scorch THE MATERIAL!" Pressing down the one-quarter-inch seam . . . very carefully . . . or the material might jump a weensy bit, making your seam crooked. Miss Jensen did not tolerate crooked seams. "Never, never a crooked seam!"

One day Miss Jensen issued us large cotton squares of material to make dish towels for the Dining Room. Holding our breath . . . concentrating on one-quarter-inch seams . . . we were on our own. Small hands, measure one-quarter inch, baste, iron.

At last it was time for sewing. Time to meet the machines of our dreams—*bad* dreams! Singer Sewing Machines. Foot pedaled. We were frightened of them.

On that day Miss Jensen took her initiates to the end of the previously forbidden hall. The long hall was highly waxed, and we stepped as though walking on crystal, afraid of slipping.

At the end of the hall, we discovered what the big key on the long gold chain opened. Miss Jensen took her time, carefully inserting the precious big key into its lock. Stepping aside she grandly opened the door. We looked in. The immense Sewing Room floor gleamed like the long hall. In its reflection we could see row after row of Singer Sewing Machines with chairs placed exactly so behind each machine.

I'd seen enough. . . . I was ready to leave. I didn't want to sew. I didn't want to do any more seams. I didn't want to go into that room.

"Step in, please," Miss Jensen said, sounding like a grand hostess.

We knew better.

We also knew . . . we'd *better*.

Miss Jensen, straight as her yardstick, sat down at a machine. We grouped around her, standing. She severely admonished us never to touch it, *her* machine.

Skillfully she demonstrated how to use the Singer—how to thread it, how to thread the bobbin, how to set the pressure foot . . . on and on and on.

Over and over she stitched.

Finally each child was assigned a machine. Our legs barely reaching the treadles.

We would try so hard in the weeks and months ahead to please Miss Jensen. But Miss Jensen was only pleased with perfect seams.

We did learn to use the machines.

Clack, clack, go slow
Clack, clack, so your
Clack, clack, cloth
Clack, clack, doesn't stretch!
Be very careful
Clack, clack

Do not make a mistake. . . . Miss Jensen might be standing behind you ready to crack your skull open with those thimbles. She had this bad little habit of beating a *rat-a-tat-tat-tat-tat* on our heads when she was displeased. She wouldn't say a word—just drill in, like a woodpecker.

Two thimbles can give you a big headache!

Besides dish towels thirty-six inches by thirty-six inches and dinner napkins twelve inches by twelve inches for the Dining Room, we sewed diapers twenty inches by twenty inches for the Hospital.

Everything we made had one-quarter-inch seams and was nearly perfect . . . thanks to Thimbles.

Holy Ghost

Like vultures they swept into our lives, tearing away bits and pieces. They wore floor-length black habits, black capes, and head coverings. Big beaded rosaries hung from their waists.

The nuns came from St. Mary's bringing Catholicism to the little heathens. They came with words such as *Heaven*, *Hell*, and *Life Everlasting*. Especially *Hell*, which seemed to be their favorite.

Our teachers were Sister Mary Angelica and Sister Mary Carmela.

Sister Mary Angelica was timid. We thought she was a bit goofy. She spoke ever so softly . . . measuring each word . . . as though afraid of making a mistake. She was forever murmuring, "Dear God, have Mercy."

Naturally we picked up on this.

"Dear God, have Mercy," we mimicked.

Sister Mary Carmela was tall, dark, and mean . . . very mean. Long hairs sprouted from her chin. She could easily have been Chief Warden at a prison such as Alcatraz or Leavenworth. There was nothing sisterly about her. With our great perceptive powers . . . we knew Sister Mary Angelica was scared of Sister Mary Carmela.

The sisters told us they were there to prepare us to be good Catholic children—to teach us our prayers and how to attend Mass in the right way.

First we were taught to make the Sign of the Cross. Repeating after Sister Mary Carmela, "In the Name of the Father . . . and of the Son . . . and of the Holy Ghost."

What? Were we hearing this right? *Ghost?*

Everything had gone smoothly until *ghost*. We had never heard of a Holy Ghost. Just ghost . . . as in ghost stories. No one wanted to say that word *ghost*. We followed correctly, but stopped at the Holy Ghost.

"We will repeat this until you get it right." Sister Mary Angelica huffed.

"Now . . . let's all make the Sign of the Cross, and say together, 'In the Name of the Father and of the Son and of the Holy . . .'"

Silence.

Big silence.

Sister Mary Carmela snapped. She went berserk!

"What's wrong with you?" she screamed, banging the table with her fists. "Can't you remember *Holy Ghost? Holy Ghost . . . Holy Ghost . . . Holy Ghost!*" Screeching it over and over. "Idiots . . . idiots . . . you WILL get this right!"

We never stirred, hiding from this hideous scene behind blank faces. *Dear God, have Mercy.*

Eventually we gave in and said it. *Ghost . . . Holy Ghost.*

We learned other new words . . . *ostracize . . . expel . . . exclude . . . excommunicate.* The Lord's Prayer and the Hail Mary were also memorized.

The only thing they didn't have to teach us was to genuflect. We thought this was fun, following the older students, copying what they did. Bobbing down . . . bending the right knee to the floor . . . popping back up . . . sliding into a pew.

Our Baptism happened on a Saturday morning in winter. We were five little girls lined up in a row before the Priest. He poured a little water on our heads, saying to each of us, "I baptize thee in the Name of the Father and of the Son and of the Holy Ghost."

We were asked if we renounced Satan, his pomp, and his works. In unison we all said a coached "I do."

The Priest gave us his blessing as we stood clasping our hands, prayerlike. I was feeling so pure and lovely . . . like an angel . . . secretly vowing never to sin. Returning to our seats, I spied the scary nuns. Sister

Mary Carmela nodding, actually smiling, taking credit for our conversion. We were trapped—that's how this had really happened. My feeling of holiness and my secret vow flew out the window.

After Baptism we were cleansed of our Original Sin they said. But there was still Venial and Mortal Sins to be dealt with . . . also First Holy Communion . . . Confirmation.

Dear God, have Mercy.

In preparation for these events were all kinds of prayers to learn. Though I tried, I didn't get them all right. Some were so frightening I didn't care to hear them let alone say them.

The one that scared the beejeebers out of me was about the gnashing of teeth and the snapping and snarling of the Devil. I didn't even understand if it was *slashing* or *gnashing* of teeth . . . but either way . . . I knew you'd be chewed to ribbons. There was a part about weeping and wailing. . . . WHO was weeping? WHO was wailing? This was heavy stuff to lay on little Natives. I didn't want to be in this scary group anymore. I wanted out!

Dear God, have Mercy.

Then we started on the Act of Contrition, being sorry for our sins. Sister Mary Carmela preached about being contrite and doing penance. She'd get to the part about "dreading the loss of Heaven and the pangs of Hell" and stare at us . . . making me so nervous. I didn't want to hear any more chilling stories about devils, fallen angels, or the eternal fires of Hell. Sister Mary Carmela reminded us constantly: "The Devil never sleeps. . . . The Devil never sleeps." She'd shake her head ominously . . . eyes flitting to the far corners of the room.

I believed she could see him.

In the beginning we had mocked Sister Mary Angelica, but now we meant it.

Dear God, have Mercy.

All that devil . . . demon . . . bad angels stuff absorbed our talks with the other little girls. I wished I could talk to my Auntie about all this. Our imaginations ran wild, affecting us so deeply that if we had to use the toilet during the night, instead of getting up and going alone as we used to do, we'd wake up whoever slept on either side. Then the three of us would slip from our beds . . . sleepwalking to the rest room.

We were always available to one another . . . no telling when YOU might have to go. You'd certainly want some guards protecting you from Satan or whatever else was roaming around or lurking in the shadows, even if your protectors were half asleep . . . 'cause the Devil never sleeps.

Now we were afraid of the dark.

Dear God, have Mercy.

Our fears continued to grow.

The Nuns emphasized over and over: "Never let a boy touch you. Never let a boy touch you."

Then: "Never let a boy touch you . . . or . . . you'll get a big belly . . . WITH A BABY IN IT!"

After that sunk in, we became deathly fearful of our boy classmates. Going to and from classes in the hallways was excruciating. The little boys walked in a group, the little girls in another, always on the alert. A boy might accidentally brush you in passing . . . and there you'd be . . . with a baby in your belly!

One of our classmates, a Mohave boy named Martin, had a paralyzed left arm and walked with a slight shuffle. He was always last in the boys' group. One morning climbing the stairs to our second-floor classroom, Martin tripped, teetering back and forth, losing his balance. As he was falling backward, his paralyzed arm flung loose, lightly grazing my shoulder. I fell backward into the other girls climbing up. It was panic time. We were tumbling all over the stairs. No one was seriously hurt. We'd just lost our footing.

I began to cry, disturbing everyone. Miss Cook, our teacher, took me to the Principal's Office. Now, Mr. Farrell, the Principal, had no patience with tears. He called a senior girl to take me back to my dormitory. I was still sniveling, but as soon as we were out of earshot, the Big Girl told me to shut up the blubbering. She had no patience either!

On entering the dormitory, Miss Bee, the Head Matron came running up. "What on earth is the matter? What's wrong?"

The Big Girl, seizing her big moment, magnified the truth. "There was this big accident on the stairs at school, and the entire third-grade class fell down the stairs on top of one another. Mr. Farrell thinks she might have some broken bones."

Hearing that I stopped sniveling and squalled as loud as possible. Mr. Farrell had said no such thing. Miss Bee gathered me up, putting me on a cot in her office.

"Now . . . now . . . don't cry anymore. Are you hurt?"

"No."

"No? Are you sure?"

"Uh, huh."

"Then please, try to stop crying." Placing a damp towel across my forehead. It made Miss Bee feel better to try and soothe me. "*Shhhhhh* . . . don't cry. . . . You're safe . . . *shhhhhh*."

I lay there sobbing . . . shuddering . . . thinking.

"Do you want me to take you to the Hospital?" she asked.

"No."

"You're going to get sick from all this crying."

"Martin . . . touched me." I could barely whisper.

"Oh, my. Did poor Martin fall too?"

"Yes." Sobbing again, "He touched me."

Very quietly Miss Bee asked, "What are you talking about? He touched you. What are you saying?"

"That Martin touched me. . . . Now I'm going to get a big belly . . . with a baby in it."

Miss Bee's speckled grey eyes looked into mine, expressing disbelief. "Who . . . told . . . you . . . this?" she demanded.

"The Sisters."

"They said this?"

"Yes."

"That's *not* true. . . . Not true at all."

She spoke sadly, gently comforting me.

All my fears came slipping out . . . the Devil . . . the bad angels . . . Hell . . . the big bellies . . . all out!

Miss Bee had heard every superstition and far-out tale imaginable from hundreds of Indian children who'd passed through her care. She was pensive and serious, saying, "When I get through with those Nuns . . . these crazy stories will stop."

Miss Bee, beautiful Miss Bee, soothed away months of ugly fears.

The tears stopped.

I didn't return to school that day. The trauma of almost having a baby had taken its toll.

Black Eyes, Bangs, and Braids

"Saturday noon I am taking you little girls to a restaurant so you can learn to order from a menu. I want to see if you have learned to use the proper silverware and just how good your manners are. I want you to trim your bangs, shine your shoes, and wear your best dresses. Above all, remember your manners!"

Speaking was the Girls' Adviser, Miss Saylor, her blue eyes flashing. Her captives were eight little Indian girls eight to nine years old. Looking so much alike . . . black eyes, bangs, and braids. We didn't dare be different.

Our dresses were cut from one pattern, the A-line, in blue denim trimmed with red or white bias tape. The only difference being small, medium, or large.

Black Eyes, Bangs, and Braids, scrubbed and shining, we were ready for our big fling. Climbing off the streetcar at Central Avenue and Washington Street someone had the misfortune to step on the heel of Miss Saylor's pump, causing it to fall off. This unforgivable clumsiness was discussed as Miss Saylor led her tiny army into the sedate Adams Hotel Dining Room.

There amid miles of tables with snowy linens, gleaming silverware, and bright crystal we were properly impressed. As we took our seats, we vowed secretly to use our very best manners, even if we were clumsy!

Miss Saylor's next instructions were: "When the Waitress brings you a menu, look it over, then order anything you like. Miss Jensen and I will take a table over there." Giving us a hard *BEHAVE* look, she left us.

We did as we were told. We ordered anything we liked.

The Waitress looked suspicious and immediately consulted Miss

Saylor. Miss Saylor flew back to our table, controlling her voice so only we could hear.

"You little idiots! Yes, I did say you could have anything you liked, but I did not mean *PIE*, *ICE CREAM*, or *CAKE*. I want you to order real *FOOD*. Now, tell the lady what you want to eat!"

Silence . . .

"Christine, you order."

Christine, scared silly, could only roll her eyes back and forth across the menu.

Big silence . . . we were all nervous.

"Eunice, you order."

"Uh . . . uh . . . uh." Poor Eunice was speechless. Miss Saylor whacked her on the shoulder.

"Eva, you order."

Cool, unfrightened Apache girl Eva replied, "French Dip Sandwich, please."

We didn't dare be different. It was French Dip Sandwich seven more times. The pressure was off. Left to ourselves again, two miracles occurred. Christine's eyes stopped rolling and Eunice's speech returned.

With a flourish of trays, the Waitress and Bus Boy arrived, deftly serving a French Dip Sandwich to each of us.

We gasped with delight at our plates—the good sandwiches and the tiny bowls of soup. We quickly picked up the tiny bowls and drank down the soup, right before Miss Saylor's eyes.

"Good God!" she hissed, heaving her huge breasts. "They drank the *au jus!*" Black Eyes, Bangs, and Braids wiggled and squirmed, casting down their eyes.

Forever printed on susceptible young minds was the terrible truth. . . . One does *not* drink *au jus* . . . however charmingly it may be served.

Arizona State Fair

Our officers began talking about November and how we'd be marching at the Arizona State Fair on Indian Day. They took us over to watch the big girls drill. We watched them, then patted ourselves on our backs, saying, "We're just as good!"

A few weeks later we went across campus to the football field to see the Boys' Companies "Passing in Review." They were experts in their drills. Their formations perfect. Their uniforms tailored to fit.

When the Indian School entertained with formal military reviews, the campus was opened to the townspeople of Phoenix. Along with the residents, wealthy winter visitors from all over the East flocked in like birds to see and talk to real Indian children. Well-trained little Natives were considered a great accomplishment on the part of the Indian Service.

The smallest boys were in Company F. These little boys under Captain Robert Lewis, a Zuni boy, trained constantly. For their efforts they earned many, many trophies . . . silver cups . . . plaques . . . ribbons. When they marched in Parade, they carried their Guidon, a large staff topped with a small brass Eagle, wings outstretched, under which fluttered numerous pennants and ribbons, awards for excellence.

The little boys executed perfection in all their drills and were captivating to watch. They resembled miniature marching military men when in fact they were children eight and nine years old.

The middle of November arrived, and the Arizona State Fair began. Thursday was established as "Indian Day." If you were Indian, you were admitted free.

On that day Indian people from tribes all over Arizona came to the

Fair. Many were relatives of ours. My own Aunt Mary, married to a Pima man named Walter Rhoads from Laveen, always came to the Fair. I'd be looking for her and my cousins.

On Indian Day all detail work was suspended. Everybody went to the Fair. By 0900 we were showered and getting into our dress uniforms—dark blue serge pleated skirt with white middie, topped off with a long navy blue scarf flipped under the collar and tied in front. Black stockings and black shoes.

At 1000 we climbed aboard the army trucks that the Arizona National Guard supplied to carry the children to the fairgrounds. It took a while to load us in.

The big event of the day began at 1100. The big event was *us!* The Phoenix Indian School showing off its regiments.

There was a huge grandstand on the west side of the Arena, decorated with red, white, and blue bunting. Flags and banners flew everywhere. We heard the Governor of Arizona speak, and all of the state officials and their families were at the Fair. There were thousands of people there to watch us . . . but to us they were one big blur.

"*Fall in!*" . . . called Captain Nona Kay in a raised voice.

We fell in.

Our lieutenants were speaking loudly, in very excited voices.

"Pay attention. . . . Keep your formations. . . . Keep your lines straight. . . . Pick up your feet. . . . Look alive. . . . Don't bunch up. . . . Pay attention!"

I could see the band way down the field. Glints of sunlight flashing off the brass horns.

"*Forward . . . march!*"

We were on our way.

Captain Nona Kay stopped us at Grandstand Center.

"*Company . . . halt!*"

People were cheering, clapping for us girls. The band was deafening.

"*Left . . . face!*" . . . facing the grandstand

"*Dress right. . . . Dress!*"

"*Right . . . face!*" . . . Snap

"*Front and center!*" . . . Snap

"*Left . . . face!*" . . . Snap

"*About . . . face!*" . . . Spin . . . backs to the grandstand

"*About . . . face!*" . . . Spin . . . face the grandstand

"*Left . . . face!*"

"*Forward . . . march!*"

Squads three and four marched right back to where we had started on the south end of the field. Somewhere in all that noise and confusion Captain Nona Kay commanded, in her tiny little voice . . .

"*To the rear. . . . March!*"

Amid the din and discord no one could hear her. So half of Company K went North and the other half went South. When she saw us marching in opposite directions, Captain Nona Kay turned squads one and two around. They double-timed, catching up with squads three and four just as we finished.

"*Company . . . halt!*"

"*Company . . . dismissed!*" Captain Nona Kay peeped.

We fell out . . . all talking at once. *Jabber . . . jabber . . . jabber . . .* laughing at ourselves for splitting up the Company. Everybody teased Company K.

At noon sack lunches were passed out, and each of us received ten tickets for the rides and sideshows.

Seeing some of the sideshow people performing on little stages in front of their tents was utterly appalling to me. I couldn't bear to look at the man with a huge snake slithering all over his body, or the tattooed man sliding a sword up and down his throat. Nor did I care to see the half man-half woman. I felt ashamed to be looking at them.

I found my cousins, and we rode the rides and went to the Agriculture Barn . . . saw the beautiful horses . . . prized cows . . . colorful chickens . . . and fluffy sheep. Then to the Home Economics Building . . . looking at quilts . . . all kinds of delicate handwork . . . prize jars of jellies . . . jams . . . fruits . . . and vegetables.

The afternoon flew by. It was 1600, 4:00 P.M. civilian time, time to climb back into the army trucks and go home.

In the Dormitory that night, the big topic of discussion among the little girls was one of the sideshow exhibits . . . a dead baby in a big glass pickle jar. The graphic description of it was horrible.

Eight years old isn't all that far from babyhood. I suppose we were all glad . . . glad . . . glad . . . that we had escaped being killed and put in a big glass pickle jar. Could have happened, you know. 'Cause it happened to that baby . . . didn't it?

Christine, Eva, and Eunice saw it!

I was glad that I hadn't.

I had seen my fill of spectacles for one day.

Old Thunder

Old Thunder, one of the little Mohave girls from Camp Verde, had this unbelievable talent—a natural ability to pass her stomach gases as she pleased. Complete control!

Sometimes when little Company K was getting dressed down for some infraction or another, instead of being smart and looking blank as the rest of us did, she showed her contempt by passing a big-time fart. I mean, high volume!

An explosion of titters would erupt within the ranks . . . causing a breakdown in discipline . . . and total exasperation from our officers. Through clinched teeth we'd murmur, "Thunder . . . Thunder."

That would set Lieutenant Polacca off. Lieutenant Mary Ann Polacca was Hopi. We were told the Hopis were the gentlest, the most docile and passive of all Native tribes. I can't imagine what ever happened to Lieutenant Mary Ann Polacca—she, of the fiery eyes and *don't give me no shit* disposition. We never got a gentle Hopi scolding from her . . . always a blistering tirade!

Lieutenant Polacca took charge, nearly slamming Captain Nona Kay aside. "I don't care if you miss lunch. . . . You are going to be *Ladies*. You are going to be *Polite*. You are going to be *Courteous*. I may just keep you here for the rest of the day."

So she began with breaking wind, children needing to control their intestinal gases and definitely not eject them anywhere, anytime one pleased! "And, those horrible unladylike burps you do . . . just to show off to each other . . . belching in each other's faces. How can you do that? It's disgusting!"

She'd bring up the craziest things, unimportant things, such as scab picking, how we'd pull scabs off our knees or elbows, making them bleed and risking infection. "I suppose you wouldn't care if they cut your leg off, just because you HAD to pick your scabs. . . . Would you?"

And, "I want that knuckle cracking stopped. . . . It causes big joints, and you'll have arthritis when you grow up . . . IF you ever grow up."

One of the worst, most repulsive things she said was "I see you snot heads, picking your noses and bringing out those boogers. Oh-h-h . . . it makes me so sick . . . I nearly throw up. Just take some toilet paper and BLOW THEM OUT!"

Talking about this made her queasy.

Ha . . . ha . . . now we knew how to make her sick!

Next she singled out the Navajo girls for their excessive gum snapping. It was true. Navajo girls were the best gum crackers in the whole world. But Lieutenant Mary Ann Polacca didn't recognize this talent. She called it *downright crude*. Demanding it stop . . . or . . . no more gum. . . . Imagine!

She continued, "All that loud, piercing screaming you little girls do. It's so shrill! I'm surprised you don't blow out your own eardrums. I'm going to give out screaming demerits any time I hear ANYONE even begin to yell. So just put a stopper in those big mouths!"

Demerits. Now this was very serious. She meant it!

Old Thunder, standing at attention like the rest of us, acted as though this tirade had nothing to do with her . . . as though she wasn't the one who brought down this scathing berating on little Company K. Staring off into space . . . not her concern . . . not her problem.

Sometimes at night when we were tucked in bed . . . on the verge of sleep . . . she'd whisper loudly, "G'nite, girls," then blast out one of her famous raspberry rips.

Old Thunder . . . signing off!

A Hey A Hey A Hey

One of the ways of working off demerits was to make cleansing powder.

Each child was given a block of pumice eight inches long, four inches wide, two-and-a-half inches thick, beige in color; an empty, clean gallon can; and some newspapers. Ground pumice became scouring powder. Its purpose was to remove stains and soap scum from showers, toilets, bathtubs, sinks, and so forth. We made this cleanser for the Big Girls' Dorm as well as our own. It required a lot to maintain both large facilities.

There was a long, narrow, cement walkway where this chore was done, and we could easily be watched . . . just in case somebody got lazy and stopped grinding or left to go play!

You'd sit on the concrete walk with a partner, legs spread with your partner's right foot on your left foot, her left foot on your right foot. In this way we braced each other, giving additional force to our chore, as we placed the brick of pumice on the cement walk, pushing it back and forth. We'd grind the brick until dust-like particles fell from it—thus making scouring powder.

Back and forth. Back and forth.

After you ground a little pile, like half a cup, you'd take a piece of newspaper, carefully sweep your little pile of powder onto the paper, then dump it into the gallon can. Repeating this over and over again, until the brick was all ground up. We ground it fine. We also ground off our fingernails. The tips of our fingers became raw.

We worked, all the time gossiping, teasing, laughing at each other and ourselves. We'd start with one partner, get tired, mutually agree to switch, sit with someone else for a while, switch again. To pass the

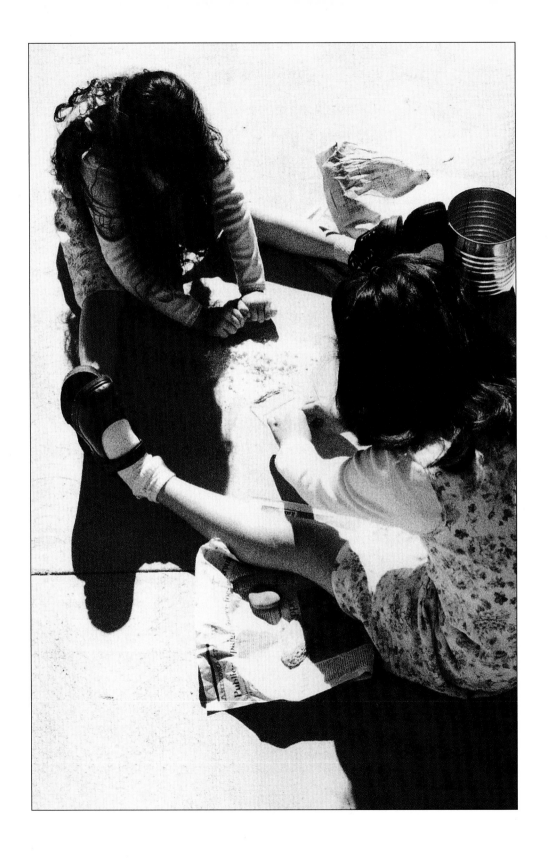

time we'd make up things, such as our little grinding song.

When someone was watching to see if we were working, whoever was facing the building and could see the spy would sing softly . . .

Hey Hey Yah
You'd better grind
Better be fine
Somebody's looking
Somebody's snooping
A Hey A Hey A Hey
If you know what's good for you
Grind, grind, grind
A Hey A Hey A Hey

Other things were made up and used in our conversations—such as *Milk Shake*. When a well-endowed big girl would run and she wasn't bound in a tight bra, if her breasts jiggled, we'd say, "Milk Shake," and fall over laughing our raunchy laughs.

There was also *Lola, Lola, Coca-Cola.*

There was a western movie star whom we knew as Lola. She had spit curls on her forehead and beside her ears and a small pouty mouth that cowboys were always trying to kiss. She'd slap them silly! We liked that. Coca-Cola referred to any voluptuous female with a curvy shape—ample breasts and hips—like a Coca-Cola bottle.

Tying our fantasies together: "Lola, Lola, Coca-Cola." With our little straight-up-and-straight-down shapes, we hoped to become Lola, Lola, Coca-Cola someday!

At 1600 we were dismissed. Slate clean. Demerits worked off—like our fingernails! Fine white powder covered our hair, eyelashes, dresses. We called each other Ghost Dancer. Screaming our joy at freedom, we'd fly off to play.

A Hey A Hey A Hey!

Wrigley Mansion

Occasionally on a Sunday afternoon during the school year, the little girls were invited to Wrigley Mansion, owned by the very Wrigleys who made the gum we chewed. Usually only the littlest girls went because the older girls had things to do, such as taking care of personal duties or spending Sunday afternoon visiting with their friends. Since personal duties were done for us little girls and we were each other's best friends, we were always ready to travel off to Wrigley Mansion with its sprawling orchard to visit and pick oranges, kumquats, whatever was in season.

Before leaving campus we'd get a good talking to.

"Use your manners. . . . Stay together. . . . Don't straggle. . . . When it's time to leave . . . leave!"

"Yes, ma'am."

"Yes, ma'am."

"Yes, ma'am."

We'd cut north through the big fields coming out at the Grand Canal. Then we'd pass Brophy College on Central Avenue, which was lined with tall old palm trees. At Camelback Road we turned east through the beautiful groves. One grove ran into another—oranges, grapefruits, lemons, olives, dates—bountiful trees laden with fruit, thick green leaves protecting them. The soft scent of blossoms always in the pure air.

The Wrigley Mansion was a white palace, perched alone on a high hill elevated above all else, surrounded completely by citrus groves. High on this knoll it was like being in the middle of a green sea. The grounds of the mansion were beautiful. Arriving at the immense gates, we'd straighten our dresses, pass a comb around so we "wouldn't look bushy," then we'd enter the palatial grounds.

We'd hear the Wrigley adults calling to one another, "The children are here. The children are here." They greeted us with affection, as their special guests. To them we were very important little people. They talked and visited with us. Always we were well received.

They introduced us to their guests. We met well-known artists, writers, musicians, movie stars. One time an Austrian Prince, another time a Grand Duchess. We were uninhibited by these famous people. We took it as a normal extension of our lives.

The time the Prince was there was unforgettable, all because of Christine the Cricket. The Prince was captivated by Christine. She had lots and lots of shiny black hair, so thick it didn't lay on her head. It sort of stood up and bounced when she moved. Her eyes were coal black and deep set. So sharp, she could pierce you with them. She was smaller than the rest of us with dark, desert coloring and very deep dimples on either side of her cheeks.

As always, we were prompted to introduce ourselves, each one telling her name and tribe to the visitors. It was always comfortable, everybody talking together.

When Christine's turn came to introduce herself, she stood up and said, "My name is Cricket and I'm from the Navajo tribe of New Mexico." Then she began giggling because this wasn't true. The visitors didn't know it, but we did. She was from the Pima tribe of Arizona. Christine thought she was so funny that she burst out laughing loudly. It got funnier and funnier to her. She couldn't stop. Tears fell down her cheeks.

The Prince thought she was delightful, urging her to come sit with him, patting a place by his side. That made Christine laugh harder. She stood there, dimples flashing, hair bouncing every which way, laughing,

laughing. Everybody had a good laugh because Christine was enjoying herself so much!

Later, we teased Eva, telling her that when she said, "I'm Eva from the great Apache tribe of Arizona," a butler fled the room and a maid fainted in fear.

Another memorable time, the younger Wrigleys were there, and they let us play with their priceless jewels . . . broaches, rings, bracelets, long strands of pearls. The young women spoke to us of quality . . . rather than quantity. They told us rubies and emeralds were preferable to diamonds, that platinum was a finer metal than even gold. They said South Sea pearls were very rare and most valuable. They showed us long, long strands that were silver grey in color. Other strands were slightly golden. I held them in my hands, feeling the Ocean flowing soft and warm through my fingertips.

They put their fine jewels on us. We didn't know how to act! We glanced at one another. Eunice had a very wide bracelet of dazzling emeralds bordered with diamonds. She carried her arm away from her body rigidly, as though in a cast. Eva was wearing the golden strands of pearls, twirling the long ends like a lasso.

"Ahem . . . Eva . . . maybe . . . you shouldn't . . . ah . . . do that . . . ah . . . maybe . . . those pearls . . . will break."

"Huh, uh . . . no . . . nope . . . they won't. Lookee, see the baby knots between each one?" She showed us, then continued twirling them.

Christine lounged in a big chair like a queen on her throne, flashing fire-red rubies on each forefinger. I knew she was imagining herself as Cleopatra. They set a heavy bib necklace of exquisite stones around my shoulders. I walked very stiff and straight. Now I was Cleopatra!

We postured. . . . We traded our jewels with one another.

For the jewels we gave up our shyness. . . . We sparkled. . . . We laughed. . . . We danced. . . . We dazzled.

A tiny gong sounded. It was teatime. We spread monogrammed linen napkins across our laps. The maids served finger sandwiches and tiny cakes on elegant Limoges china. We drank lemonade from tall Waterford glasses. Slowly, we nibbled our treats, luxuriating in this hospitality.

The tiny gong sounded again. Time to go. Remembering our instructions, "When it's time to leave . . . leave!"

They handed us small packets of candies and gum, telling us to return soon. Quickly saying thank you and good-bye, we left.

These wealthy people took time for us, little Indian children, and made us feel special. They enriched our lives far beyond anything they ever imagined.

After these visits, we'd scurry home with our candies and heavy bags of fruit we'd picked earlier in the afternoon. Sometimes someone's bag would burst open, scattering oranges all over, or a bag of fruit became too heavy to carry any farther and was left by the road.

Eventually we learned to wait until we were nearly home to pick fruit, going into an orchard and helping ourselves. People encouraged this, as the fruit was always going to waste.

Arriving back at school, we were given "sack lunches" for our supper. We'd be exhausted by then—jumping into showers, into nightgowns, and into bed—contented and pleased with the day, fast asleep by dusk.

Apache Girls

They decided to leave. Just like that. These two young Apache girls. They were homesick for their parents, lonesome for their homeland. So . . . they left.

No one knew when they went. They weren't discovered missing until 9:00 P.M. bed check. That's the time Companies G, H, I, and J went to bed.

You wouldn't believe the awful commotion when they were reported missing. The matrons, the company captains, the lieutenants, the secondary officers, all clomping around, yelling, ordering each lesser officer around. Opening and searching the girls' empty lockers. Banging them shut. Opening and slamming them shut again and again, as though the Apaches might turn up in there. Then they'd yell up to us in the sleeping quarters . . . "You little girls better stay in bed and go back to sleep!"

Sleep . . . with this commotion?

"Stay off the stairs too."

Later . . . "This doesn't concern you!"

Or . . . "If I have to come up there . . ."

Then Miss Saylor and Mr. Durham, the Boys' Disciplinarian, arrived, and all hell broke loose. Loud threats were made about what would happen to "those Apache Girls when we catch them."

Miss Saylor would give them enough demerits so they'd never be able to leave campus again . . . ever. Even when they got old they'd still be working off demerits. They'd still be scrubbing . . . floors . . . toilets . . . sinks . . . walls . . . on and on and on. I knew Mr. Durham would beat them unconscious.

The craziness continued. They brought in big floodlights to spray

light over this great Kaffir cornfield just west of the Little Girls' Building.

All night this light swept endlessly over and across the field. The big boys were brought in to go through the huge cornfield to look for the girls . . . like in a rabbit hunt with the hunters walking in a line and the scared rabbits jumping out.

Lined up at the wide screened-in windows were barefoot little girls in long nightgowns . . . watching and hoping the Apache girls weren't in the Kaffir cornfield.

Now, why would the Apache girls go west when their homeland was in the other direction, we asked one another.

They fled east.

They made it home.

However, the Superintendent of their agency returned them to Phoenix Indian School. They did not want to be back. Their parents did not want to send them back. But the government ruled our lives, and the Superintendent was the government.

When they were returned, the Apache girls weren't given demerits. . . . They weren't beaten. What hideous thing happened was this: For punishment their beautiful, waist-long black hair was cut off . . . then their heads were shaved bald.

Who did this repulsive thing to them? We never heard.

Thereafter, they wore tams or scarves to hide their baldness. From then on they never played or mixed with other girls.

They withdrew.

They were alone . . . together.

These were nice, kindly girls, good students, who just got homesick.

After that school term ended, we never saw the Apache girls again.

Lola, Lola, Coca-Cola

The trolley swung right onto Washington Street, the main drag. We little girls perked up, sliding across the aisle and taking seats on the south side of the car, preparing for the action ahead.

We were coming up the long block we called "The Forbidden Land." All the businesses were on the south side of the street. There were no storefronts to the north.

The Boys' Disciplinarian, Mr. Durham, often lectured, "The Indian students must NEVER leave the streetcar here. This area is strictly off-limits to the Indian students."

The Girls' Adviser, Miss Saylor, in her unwelcome sermon to us before leaving campus, reminded us that this zone was the gathering place of "trashy women, bad men, and old flappers."

The nuns who taught us catechism said, "As an act of love, just shut your eyes and say Hail Marys for those poor souls as you pass through their area."

The big girls whispered that this long block was called "The Red Light District." We hadn't the faintest idea what that meant. But we knew it meant something—because everyone preached about this part of Washington Street.

As we approached, the saloons and pool halls came into view. They were doing a big Saturday business.

We held our breath.

Then . . . there they were . . . the fancy ladies . . . all dolled up . . . strutting along the street! Oh, mercy, *ohhhh*.

We weren't interested in the men who hung around in small groups, smoking, leering, joshing. It was the striking ladies we wanted to see, in their tight dresses, high-heeled shoes, and silk stockings with black seams up the backs of their legs. Their painted faces . . . white face powder . . . red cheeks . . . red lips . . . thick mascara on their eyelashes. Kinda flirty, kinda scary!

Ummm, ummm, ummm, la de dah. Low down trashy ladies!

"Lola, Lola, Coca-Cola," we said to one another, giggling, wicked glints in our eyes.

Secretly, we each imagined ourselves as one of them. Then we said it aloud.

"That's you, Christine, in the shiny black dress."

"Not me . . . huh, uh . . . I'm the one in those orange high heels, with straps going around my ankles."

"Ohhhhhhhh, look at the one in the red dress. It's so tight, it's gonna split open."

"That's me! That's my red dress."

"Eunice, you can barely wiggle in your dress."

"I'm the one with those scary black false eyelashes . . . and that long cigarette."

Close our eyes and pray? And miss these gorgeous ladies? No way, Sister Mary Angelica.

Now and then the saloon's bat-winged doors would swing open. But the trolley passed by so fast we could never see in.

We heard the loud music blaring from the establishments. "La Cucaracha" and "La Paloma" were the hit songs. We heard guitars, horns, and drums. Thinking what grand times they must be having in the saloons and wondering why the fancy ladies weren't inside dancing to "The Cockroach" or "The Dove."

The tram rattled on, Mr. Conductor clanging his bell.

"Goldwater's," he called out.

All sinful thoughts fell away as we slipped down into Goldwater's fairyland basement. Goldwater's had the most exclusive basement in all the West. We felt rich and important just entering it. The pleasure of looking at lovely, marked-down items was all ours. It was all we could do . . . just look . . . and plot.

"Someday I'm going to have this," we promised one another. "Someday I'm going to buy that." Someday.

My buying generally centered on small boxes of handkerchiefs. Three to a box. Each little handkerchief made a nice gift for a friend who could not make it to town. Before making my selection, I would study them all carefully . . . the beautiful embroidery and the bit of lace on one corner . . . the teeny stickers that said, "Made in France." Solemnly I made my purchase, counting out the nickels and dimes. Ninety-eight cents.

After Goldwater's it was on to Kress's. They had everything—jewelry, fake diamonds and pearls, housewares, hairpins, pink hair-waving lotion, Evening in Paris perfume, dresses, underwear, shoes, on and on.

At Kress's there was a long lunch counter where we ordered milk shakes and a candy counter that had licorice whips, marshmallow babies, Boston beans, horehound, and jelly beans in bulk. For ten cents we stuffed ourselves.

Should we want to go to a movie in town, there was the New Fox Theater or the Rialto on Washington Street. Around the corner one block north was the Grand Orpheum Theatre. It was there our teacher, Miss Osborne, had taken a small group of us to see the distinguished actor John Barrymore in a Shakespearean play, *The Merchant of Venice*. "This will improve and upgrade your lives," she said. But nothing at all happened—probably because I didn't understand a word they said.

At the corner of Washington Street and Central Avenue in front of Walgreens we visited with the gentle, soft-spoken Pima women who sat on small blanket pallets on the sidewalk. In their plain cotton dresses, tan lisle hose, and sturdy oxfords, and their dark hair braided down their backs, each woman was a study in quiet grace and dignity.

Spread before them on pieces of white cloth lay their beautiful black-on-red pottery. They sold these exquisite pieces for just twenty-five cents to five dollars.

These women were so kind, asking us about school, understanding it as yet another reality to be dealt with. They cautioned us to behave well . . . to learn all we could . . . to be good to one another.

By late afternoon it was time to leave town. We had to be checked in at school by 5:00 P.M. at the latest. If you took the 4:00 P.M. trolley, you were home safe. However . . . since we little girls lived on the edge . . . we caught the 4:30 P.M. trolley.

Tired, satiated from the town, we climbed aboard our trolley marked "Indian School."

Mr. Conductor asked, "Well, girls, did you enjoy yourselves?" Adding, "Now don't worry, I'll get you back in time so's you won't get them damn ol' demerits!" Then he slammed the doors shut and hammered down on his bell.

Clang . . . clang . . . clang!

We shot out of town . . . traveling fast . . . the little trolley swaying all over the rails.

This was the time to pray!

Oh God, please don't let us be late. . . . Please, don't let us get demerits. . . . Oh God, if this trolley jumps off the tracks and kills us, please take me straight to Heaven where I belong. Spare me from Purgatory where Sister Mary Angelica says I'm bound.

We clung tightly to our seats.

Then . . . the trolley screeched to a halt. Metal grinding metal.

"Indian School . . . end of line."

Doors flew open and we flew out, yelling over our shoulders, "Thank you, Mr. Conductor."

We ran as fast as we could to the Main Office.

Miss Saylor was waiting, elegantly dressed, seated at her desk. The big Waterbury clock on the wall ticked loudly as if it were saying . . . *Late . . . late . . . late.*

But we weren't, barely squeaking in by our 5:00 P.M. curfew. Risking demerits and long hours of working them off.

We hurriedly checked off our names on the "list of town girls," trying to slip out of the office as quickly as possible.

"Come back here," Miss Saylor commanded. Striving to trap us, trying to sound casual, she asked, "Did you . . . see . . . those . . . trashy . . . painted-up . . . women . . . in town?"

Eunice: "No, ma'am."

Wide-eyed Christine: "Nothing. I didn't see any of them."

Eva: "I shut my eyes."

What? Yeah sure, and you prayed too, Eva—you ol' flapper!

Miss Saylor was making us crazy.

Miss Saylor was making us little liars.

We were making ourselves little survivors.

Homecoming

Journey Home

It was the day before Christine, Eva, Eunice, and I would be scattered to distant reservations. We were going home from school. We clung to one another, promising to be back at the end of August. This had been a difficult year with so much to learn and a new way of living, but we had survived. This afternoon we did what we knew was the proper way to treat friends—we had a give-away, giving one another tiny presents. My give-away was a small sack of candies for each one. Christine gave me a hair clip, Eunice a hankie, and Eva a brass safety pin.

Saying . . . good-bye . . . I'll see you in August. . . . You better be back. . . . Be back!

―――

The next day the students were up at 4:00 A.M. After a quick breakfast we went directly to the Big Girls' Dorm. Parked in front were two Greyhound buses. We boarded immediately, joined by other students heading to our part of the country. We were going to reservations in Northern Arizona and Eastern New Mexico.

Early that afternoon we said good-bye to the Hopi students who left us in Tuba City, Arizona. The rest of us traveled on to a small Indian School in Cameron, Arizona, where we spent the night. There, many of the Navajo students said their good-byes. We had a swim in the pool before supper, then to bed.

The following day we were up again at 4:00 A.M. for the end of our long journey. By this time only one bus was needed. The newness of traveling so far in a big bus and the exhilaration of being with all these other children, outside of school, was wearing me out.

There was a sack lunch stop to stretch and eat a sandwich. Then we were off again.

Finally the big Greyhound bus, its brakes bucking and screeching, shuddered to a complete stop. We were in the Santa Fe railroad parking lot in Gallup, New Mexico.

"Stay in your seats until the luggage is out," the Bus Driver shouted back to us.

Peering out the windows I saw a big group of Indian parents standing around, waiting for this bus and the return of their beloved children.

The Zuni women were richly clad in black mantas and white buckskin-wrapped moccasins. Navajo ladies wore velvet shirts, studded with old coins from the 1800s, and exquisite turquoise jewelry. The men wore bright shirts.

Quietly we stepped off the bus.

Gently parents gathered children in their arms, murmuring soft, sweet words in their ears.

When I saw my Father . . . I was surprised at how handsome he looked . . . in his red cotton shirt, Levis, boots, and a tan Stetson. Around his hips was a heavy silver Concho belt. I'll never forget how he looked that day.

When I left for school so many months ago, I could barely stand to look at him, thinking he was ugly and mean.

Now I understood a bit more of life.

This man was my Father and he had sent me away to the best place he knew because he couldn't care for me and do his job.

Now I could put aside the bad feelings.

"My Daughter . . . my child," he said.

My eyes filled with tears. I didn't know how much I'd missed this life until I saw it again. The other children lifted their heads higher, straightened their shoulders with the same proud feelings.

I knew our thoughts were similar.

These are my people . . . my beautiful Native relatives. This is who I am. . . . I am one of them!

———

Crown Point was sixty-five miles away. My Father threw my suitcase in the back of his pickup and we were off. As we rode along, I gulped in fresh clean air scented with Juniper and Cedar.

Endless mesas blazing in endless colors, farther than my eyes could see. Shadows were stretching long. Shepherds herded their flocks home for the night.

We came up over Lone Mesa. Spread out below lay the tiny village of Crown Point. To the north was Rattlesnake Mesa. To the south, the Hawk's Eye. Seeing these familiar landmarks made my feet itch, wanting to get back on trails that took us to special places and unforgettable times.

We went straight to Aunt Elizabeth's. We entered through the kitchen and . . . yum, yum, yum . . . I could smell posole burbling in its pot. On the table were loaves of fresh baked Pueblo bread. A big feast tonight!

Out on the porch they were gathered, waiting for us—Aunt Elizabeth, Uncle Joe, Lucy Brown, Mr. and Mrs. Ance, and my dear friends . . . Naneh and Little Fat.

Auntie scooped me into her arms. Now . . . I was home. Then Uncle Joe picked me up, saying I'd gained fifty pounds!

I shook hands with the other adults, then Naneh, Little Fat, and I just stood there together . . . awkward. Not knowing what to say or how to say it. Aware the adults' big eyes were on us. Smiling shy smiles at one another . . . bashful . . . tongue-tied . . . all three of us!

Spread out on the floor was the familiar old yellow Elk Skin. On this very large skin was a black pottery bowl filled with Cedar. Uncle's Eagle Fan was placed to the side, and his small medicine pouch lay on top of the fan.

Uncle Joe, in his wonderful broken English, welcomed me home. Picking up the little pouch he offered me a pinch of Sacred Yellow Corn Pollen.

"You know wha' t'do," he said.

Yes, certainly I'd not forgotten this important Ceremony. I took the Sacred Yellow Corn Pollen as my beautiful Grandmother had taught me so long ago.

While I was doing that, my Father lit the Cedar. Blowing his breath on it, he handed the black bowl to Aunt Elizabeth, who blew her breath on it. Uncle Joe took the black pottery bowl, the Cedar now barely smoking. Waving his Eagle Fan over the Cedar, he blew his breath on it. Then Uncle Joe covered the bowl with his fan and spoke.

"This child was eight years ole when she went to a far-away place, all alone to get education. We are heppy our lil one is home. But furs she needs to rid of anytin' bad, ugly, or mean that she may have experience over there. So, smokin' down wit pure Cedar will take care of it. While I am purifyin' my Niece, get ready to take some for yourself."

I'd forgotten how pungent Cedar smoke was. I'd also forgotten how fine it was to have a splendid Ceremony given to you.

After we were fanned down, the lingering Cedar scent clung to our skin. We smelled of fresh Rain . . . of vast Deserts . . . of high Mesas . . . of red-purple Sunsets . . . of the Creator's Earth.

Speaking to all of us, Aunt Elizabeth said, "I've prepared a little meal of good Indian food with Pueblo bread. Come now, let's all eat and enjoy this homecoming feast."

At the words . . . *food . . . bread . . . feast . . .* time fell away between Naneh, Little Fat, and me.

We immediately began making big plans for the next day. Should we climb Rattlesnake Mesa . . . or borrow Grey Eyes's team and wagon?

Hey!

Beauty Way

Leaving in late afternoon to attend a small sing several miles away, Naneh, Little Fat, and I traveled quickly, taking shortcuts over the Mesa. We were in a hurry to see our friends. On our return home we'd take the longer, safer trails back.

Our destination tonight was the Antonios' compound. Their hogans and sheep corrals were nestled against a small canyon wall blended into the Earth, nearly invisible. As we approached, the sheep with their tender bleating let us know where they were penned. The ferocious sheepdogs bounded out to eat us, but were whistled back.

The Antonio family was having a Beauty Way Ceremony for their eldest son, Willetto. He had been away for a long while, living in one of the metropolitan cities of the Southwest. Now, on returning home, Willetto felt a need to relieve his mind and spirit of the city's pressures . . . anxieties . . . cares.

It was of the utmost importance that he be returned to Harmony with himself and all else in the Universe. To walk again in the Beauty Way.

Before stepping into the clearing, we straightened our clothing, patted down our hair, and wiped our moist faces on our sleeves. Our arrival was in the coolness of dusk. We were greeted warmly by the host family.

Since this was a small Ceremony, only family members and a few friends gathered. We were there because of our families' relationships with these people. They told us to make ourselves comfortable; and we sat down and rested, making small talk. They offered us cool, pure spring water from gourd dippers. It was sweet and good.

After we were rested, Nezbah, Willetto's sister, invited us to the

Ceremony Hogan. We followed her in and slid down onto the dirt floor that was lavishly covered with thick sheepskin hides. The hogan was dark, lighted by the smallest of flames in the center.

No conversation here . . . Naneh, Little Fat, and I sitting to the side quietly observing. As our eyes adjusted, we could see them. Willetto was lying on a luxurious pallet of skins and robes. The Medicine Man was dressed so beautifully . . . blue velvet shirt, large Concho belt, bow guard on his left wrist, turquoise necklace with joclas. A white silk headband held his greying hair in place. He wore red moccasins.

I became aware of the other people, three of them. Adults, sitting motionless against the opposite wall. In the dim, flickering firelight, they looked unreal. I felt little shivers. . . . I wondered if they were from here or another realm. . . . I kept looking . . . looking sideways . . . looking without moving my head. The little flame blazed up momentarily. Then I recognized Old Slim Man, who was one of Willetto's relatives.

The Medicine Man was chanting, using a small gourd rattle filled with tiny crystals from the Underworld. They were brought up by the Ant People from their palaces far beneath the Earth . . . to sparkle and glisten . . . atop their hills.

He sang . . . our hearts sang

Time has no meaning in Ceremony

The moment lasts indefinitely

We were in that moment

Into infinity we were there

Belonging to the Beauty Way

On leaving the Ceremony Hogan, we went to the brush Cedar arbor where the ladies were cooking. Again a little visiting . . . mostly we answered questions. The Antonio ladies fed us rich mutton stew with fry bread and sweet, sweet coffee. We ate with restraint. We were young . . . trying to act grown up.

Then it was time . . . leaving time. . . . Morning Star had already begun his journey across the Great Sky.

Handshakes all around

Just touch the fingers

Softly

Good morning . . . Good life

I loved those long walks back. No shortcuts. Following foot trails onto dirt roads. Luminous stars . . . blazing through the Universe.

The silence of the desert broken only by night birds' caressing calls. Old Warrior Coyotes singing in distant canyons.

Naneh, Little Fat, and I were serious and sober, beginning to realize the truths of the peoples' teachings.

Had we not witnessed an exquisite Ceremony?

Weren't our very beings filled with its melody?

Our senses moved on a higher level. . . . We were safe.

In beauty I walk

With beauty before me I walk

With beauty behind me I walk

With beauty above me I walk

With beauty around me I walk

Walk in beauty

Walk in beauty

Walk in beauty

Walk in beauty

Epilogue

Long years later, thirty some, in fact, we once again packed peanut butter sandwiches and climbed Rattlesnake Mesa . . . to look for the last time at The Great Snake. The Winds . . . the Rains . . . the Snows . . . had only made it more beautiful. Time does that . . . you know. Bidding a joyous farewell to the Land we so honored and loved, Naneh, Little Fat, and I sprinkled Sacred Pollen out into the Universe. The Land in turn gave us its gentle release. It had already given us Adventures . . . Strength . . . Resilience. *Aho*.

THE JOURNEY TO
Rattlesnake Mesa
Stories from a Native American Childhood

EdNah New Rider Weber and Richela Renkun share a special relationship. Several years ago they met through a mutual friend and quickly developed a unique bond that led them on a remarkable journey together.

In 1998, the two set out to revisit the landscape of Weber's childhood in New Mexico—searching for old memories and creating new images to recapture them. Covering territory Weber had not visited since the 1930s, some landmarks remained while others had to be sought after with an archaeologist's eye. They discovered crumbled adobe foundations and walkways hidden beneath years of overgrown brush and grasses. They searched for faces of children and elders who were part of the land, faces that helped Weber remember the people she had known in her youth.

Weber and Renkun's journey became a moving ceremony in itself—with prayers, tears, and laughter all along the way.